BLACK PEARLS

BLACK PEARLS

True-life adventures and a historical quest by the man who cast himself and his family away on an island paradise

Tony Williams

<u>Genesis</u>

First published in Great Britain by Genesis, 2000

Genesis
114 Whitchurch Road
Cardiff
CF14 3LY

ISBN: 0-9535202-3-4

Typeset by:
QueerTypes
Hebron
Whitland
Pembrokeshire
SA34 0XX

Printed and bound in Great Britain
by Gomer Press, Llandysul, Ceredigion

To the memories of Kauraka Kauraka,
Tapu Richard and Ron Powell.

Acknowledgements

I could not have written this book without the help of many people, among them Cook Island News for their invaluable information on the devastation caused by Hurricane Martin; Ora Moana Pearls and Cook Islands Federation of Pearls for permission to use the photo on the front cover; my friends in the Cook Islands for their help and support during the writing of this book; and Andy for his help.

Contents

Introduction

'Travel, in the younger sort, is a part of education; in the elder, a part of experience.' The words are those of Francis Bacon in his essay, 'Of Travel'.

I have been lucky enough to experience both of those benefits of travel. I've been educated, and I've certainly gained experience.

This book is a distillation of my travels – some of which can be read of in my other books, *Island of Dreams* and *The Forgotten People*. The former tells of how I and my family deliberately cast ourselves away on a desert island. The latter tells of a different journey, made in an attempt to prove the link between my native Wales and the Mandan tribe of Native Americans.

In *Black Pearls* I make another journey – a journey once again to my beloved Cook Islands. I say 'my', because the Cooks hold a very special place in my heart. Maina is a very small island that became our paradise, when my wife Cathy, my children Matthew, Stacey and Craig and I suffered hurricanes and sunburn, lived on fish and coconuts, and entertained two men from the *Mirror* newspaper – both of them called Harry.

I couldn't keep away from the islands after that, and have returned since. During my visits, I have learned a lot about the Cook Islanders' way of life – and not all of it makes for pleasant retelling. Around the narrative of our experiences as castaways and our search for the link between an American Indian tribe and a Welsh prince I weave the story of Miari, she of the silken hair, the smooth, flawless skin and the huge brown eyes.

Hers isn't always a happy story. She tells me of sexual abuse as a child, of making ends meet, of survival in a large family, of broken relationships. Yet she carries these burdens with a happy-go-lucky *joie de vivre* that most of us would die for.

While I spent long balmy hours with Miari – clinging to the back of her 100cc motorbike, relaxing on one of the many tiny islets, or *motus* – I had time to reflect on the months I had spent with my family on Maina, baking in the sun, and on the freezing desert nights spent in North Dakota, sleeping in a tent or under the stars.

I also speak to survivors of the devastating Cyclone Martin, which had such a catastrophic effect on the lives of Cook Islanders.

Much of what you will read in these pages is through the words of those with stories to tell. Miari's distinctive voice and earthy and casual delivery cannot fail to paint a picture in your mind. Nor can the voices of the Mandan Native Americans in North Dakota, who tell of how the government deprived them of large parts of their homeland in order to build a dam, of how at school they were forbidden to use their native language or dress in their traditional way.

All the voices you will 'hear' in *Black Pearls* create vivid, spirited images of lives that are a thousand times removed from the culture most of us are accustomed to. You will read the story of Teretia Piniata, who told me, '[Cyclone Martin] hit the island so fast, I was more amazed at everything than scared.' And Mairi Samson's story: 'We didn't expect that Martin would totally destroy everything on the island. All the houses have been flattened down.'

Then there's Bernice's story. She is a Mandan Indian, and tells us of the time their reservation was inundated to make a dam for the white man: 'The army engineers came and cut all the wood off. We didn't have anything, not even a stick for firewood. They cut all the trees, then they flooded the area. They made us all move up to higher ground. Now the whole land is all flooded.'

These are people whose lives have been affected – sometimes devastated – by natural phenomena and man-made circumstances alike, and I am indebted to them for their readiness to talk to a complete stranger from Wales with his little hand-held tape recorder, who managed to capture their joy and their anger as they related to me those episodes in their lives that will remain in their memories for ever. I hope I have done justice to their testimonies in this book.

I have brought these stories together in *Black Pearls*,

because I am both Bacon's 'younger sort' and elder man, and I want to give you a taste of what both educated me and gave me experiences I'll never forget.

1

In Captain Cook's Footsteps

The Cook Islands are a scattering of fifteen islands spread over nine hundred miles (1,450 kilometres) of ocean where the sun always shines. Of the southern group of eight islands, Rarotonga is the biggest, the most populous and lively, and is mountainous and volcanic and fertile. Lying 2,100 miles (about 3,400 kilometres) northeast of New Zealand, it consists of steep forested mountains, rock formations and a waterfall in the middle, with a ring of plantations and villages and beaches round the edge.

There are two main roads: the new one, closer to the beach, which goes right round the island, and the old inner circle road, which was originally made of coral. The two-roomed hut I had rented was conveniently situated between the two.

It was a small and compact building, one room of which contained a cooker, a table with two chairs, a small fridge and a bed. The other room contained the shower and toilet. The hut was surrounded by lush vegetation, fruit trees and tropical flowers of all shapes – splashes of red and yellow, pink and purple, blue and white all about me. I could have been in the garden of Eden for all anybody knew.

I settled down on the veranda. The sky here was a distillation of blue, the ideal of blue. There were no shades in it, no hesitations or doubts: it was endlessly, solidly blue. Yet when you stared up at it you could never find the source of the blueness, the part where the world ended and heaven began.

I was absorbed in this place, having returned year after year since 1989, each time spending no less than a few months.

I had met Miari on my last visit. She was a beautiful island dancer, who had many friends and many more admirers, yet she struck me as a very lonely person. She was to visit me later in the day; it had been a year since our last meeting.

I husked a coconut for a refreshing drink, while I waited for her arrival.

On previous visits I'd worn veritable blinkers and hadn't really got to know the people – those lucky people who lived in paradise. I had been on a soul-searching mission, for my inner self, the meaning of my existence. Whenever I returned to Britain I always felt I'd left a part of myself behind. I had spent a lot of time cast away on the remote islands, fishing and living off the land, in search of my own identity.

As the years passed, I began to spend more time on the

main island of Rarotonga, getting to know the people – Miari especially. I felt a bond with her, a connection, if you like – and I had a feeling that, like me, she too was in search of something, something that perhaps was never really there.

Miari hadn't changed. I watched her as she approached the hut. She must have been in her mid-twenties. I made my approach from the veranda, as she dismounted the scooter she'd been riding. Suddenly we were wrapped in each other's arms, in a welcoming hug.

'Peea ua Koe?' I said, using some local Maori I'd picked up on my last visit. Miari began to laugh and replied,

'Meitaki maata.' Roughly translated, the exchange between us was: 'How are you?' 'Very good, thank you.'

It was an extremely hot day, even for the Cook Islands, but Miari all in black in her shorts and crop-top, looked cool and unaffected by the intense heat, which was being radiated unmercifully by the afternoon sun. Miari obviously felt hotter than she looked, for she suggested that we go to the waterfall for a swim – or, in my case, a paddle.

It was no mean task, two adults on a 100cc motor scooter climbing the high hill of the jungly interior, zigzagging to avoid the fallen coconut husks that were strewn haphazardly across the path that led to the waterfall.

After the uphill obstacle course, we eventually reached our destination. The waterfall was cradled between surrounding formations of rock that were covered with foliage.

The water cascaded through the centre of the rocks, creating an ideal pool for the islanders to cool off in.

I sat on the ground and watched as Miari stood underneath the glistening waterfall. As she let down her hair, which had been tied up in a tight knot above her head, it fell down to just below her thighs, and, like the cascading water, it clung to her body, caressing her, until she finally made her descent into the water below.

I wasn't so lucky: the only thing that clung to me were the mosquitoes – swarms of them. This area was their breeding ground, owing to the wet and warm conditions. They were hungry for my blood – *my blood*! Luckily these were non-malaria-carrying mosquitoes or else I would be in a lot of trouble. I sat there slapping at my arms and legs, like a one-man band but without instruments.

The sun was starting to go down. As Miari emerged from the water, she was like the proverbial poetry in motion. She walked towards me, and I couldn't help but feel a kind of passion, not just for her, also for the beauty of this place. Of course I'd learned over the years that this was not paradise to everyone: for some of the people of this island the lifestyle I was trying to escape from was their idea of paradise.

I didn't feel that this was the right place to hear Miari's story: for one thing, the mosquitoes were driving me crazy; and another reason was that it was becoming quite dim and I didn't fancy our chances of getting down the littered path in the dark. We did, however, make it back safely to solid ground.

We eventually decided to go back to my humble abode, and by the time we'd reached it the sun had already dropped over the horizon, leaving the sky with all the violent colours of a bruise. Miari settled into one of my cane chairs, and set about plaiting her silky jet-black hair. I was tempted to ask if I could do it for her, but decided it wouldn't be a very good idea. Making some coffee was a much safer bet.

Miari seemed to have a certain effect on many members of the male gender: I'd seen heads turn and men of all ages go weak if she so much as smiled in their direction. She was the ultimate dusky maiden who could even tempt the Pope if she turned on the charm, which was something she wasn't short of.

I handed Miari her coffee and settled in the chair opposite. 'This is cosy,' she remarked, and then added, 'I always feel comfortable around you Tony. You never expect anything.' It must be hard for a woman like Miari, to trust any man. To most it was a case of lust at first sight, especially if their first encounter was while Miari was working.

Being a traditional island dancer had its drawbacks: always having to smile at the audience, while at the same time shaking her hips quite suggestively, sometimes at a great speed, causing droplets of sweat to run an erotic path down her oiled body. It was at one of these island nights that I had been introduced to Miari. A friend, who was also a friend of Miari, thought that I'd be interested in hearing her story. We got on great: we had a lot in common and talked for hours.

I walked her home that night. I often wondered whether this beautiful young woman was putting herself in danger every time she walked home in the dark. I just seemed to sense vulnerability about her, an almost childlike quality.

I said goodnight when we reached her place, but was quite taken aback when she gave me the biggest smile and hugged me tight. 'What was that for?' I asked. I was even more surprised when she said, 'When you offered to fetch me home, I thought you wanted to fuck me! But I should have realised after our conversation tonight, that you weren't like the rest of the *papaas* [white men].'

It made me wonder whether that was the view of all the islanders – that all Europeans came here for was to take. I hoped that wasn't the case.

I thought about my past and was convinced that it had always been my destiny to join the list of British men who loved these islands. I had read and reread the passage about the famous mutiny in Captain Bligh's book. In 1789, two weeks after the *Bounty* left the Cook Islands, Fletcher Christian and his friends were cast adrift with some of the crew. When Bligh tried to work out why the mutiny had happened, he concluded that it was because so many of the men had fallen in love with women on Tahiti and had been welcomed by the islanders.

Under these, and many other attendant circumstances, equally desirable, it is now perhaps not so
much to be wondered at ... that a set of sailors,
most of them void of connections, should be led
away; especially when, in addition to such powerful inducements, they imagined it in their power
to fix themselves in the midst of plenty, on one of
the finest islands in the world, where they need
not labour, and where the allurements of dissipa-
tion are beyond anything that can be conceived.

This passage supported the arguments I had started to
have in my own mind. I was 'void of connections'. I had
everything to live for here and nothing in Wales. Here was
family, warmth, freedom – everything that Britain had
failed to offer me.

Miari looked relaxed, so I turned on my recorder and
began to tape her story.

'How did you get into professional island dancing?' I
asked.

'Well, it wasn't until I came back to Raro[tonga] to
live, at about sixteen, that I joined a local dance troop,' she
began. 'I thought: Yeah this would be a good way to settle
back into island life. I'd lived most of my life up until then
in New Zealand, because my auntie brought me up. It's
kind of a way of life for Cook Islanders: if another member
of the family wants to bring up a child, then more often
than not the parents give them that child. Yeah, that's how
it is here.

'The main reason I came back was because my best
friend, who I'd grown up with and who was more like a

sister to me, was dying of cancer. I just couldn't handle it, man. We'd done everything together: we discovered alcohol and boys and all that stuff. When I found out her illness was terminal I just freaked out and left Raro. It was shortly after that I met a guy, a local. He was nice – or at least I thought so at the time, but I was pretty inexperienced because, you know, I didn't really think I would get into that kind of stuff. But we went out a couple of times. He was my first sexual experience.

'I remember thinking: Is that it? There was no enjoyment: the only thing I felt was let down. What a joke! Then he two-timed me and so I dumped him.

'Then I spent six months in Japan with the dance troop, and when we returned I decided to go back to New Zealand. I felt more independent. I wanted to be with my friend and help her during her time of need. She died in hospital several months later. I still remember that night, hearing her coughing, being woken up by the nurse who was shaking me and telling me that my friend was calling for me. I jumped up and ran into her room, just catching her last gasp of air. She looked so different from the pretty, happy-go-lucky girl I'd grown up with. She was all yellow and skinny and lifeless, with her mouth wide open and her eyes just – just staring.

'I'll never forget the way she looked that day. I wasn't exactly scared – it didn't click until I phoned my mum to tell her that Ria had passed away that I burst into tears, 'cos I didn't know how to explain it. She's gone, she's gone away, and it was like, "What do you mean?" It's like she's gone, man.'

After going home and having a shower, then returning to the hospital, Miari and members of Ria's family set to work bathing the corpse. It was a memory that will remain with her.

'It wasn't until we flipped her over and she was like a board, you know, stripped naked, skinny like as a board – that was when I snapped.'

Miari paused, considering the story she had just imparted to me.

'I thought the nurses did that,' I said.

'Well, they do,' she said, 'but the family wanted to do it. It's our way, you know – how we show our respect. But I just snapped and walked out of the room. And her father, man – it's actually her stepfather: her mother married a *papaa* – he's such a wanker, man. I hate his guts. Anyway, we were not allowed to see Ria. They just kept her away from us. He made sure the funeral was short and sweet. In our tradition we kinda like keep the box open at home, you know, in the lounge. Everybody comes pay their respects, you know – mourn and mourn and mourn – and a week after go and bury them. We can't do that over in Raro because they have nowhere to refrigerate them, so they have to bury them immediately. But over there in New Zealand they keep them in the morgue, or in the house for a few days, and then take them back to the morgue, and then bring them out and then bury them. So you can grieve and grieve over the person until they are buried, and then it's OK. But Ria's was so quick, and we didn't really feel like we had gotten over it, because it was so quick. It's like: she died, the following day, funeral, and then – bang! – back to

normal life. I really hated his guts man: he's such a domi-
nating person.'

Miari barely drew breath before moving on to the next
phase of her young life, so keen was she to relate her story.

'Anyway,' she continued, 'then I flew to Raro, then to
Japan, and in Japan I met this guy – I met this Japanese.
He was such a good friend of the [dance] group and he'd
take us out quite often. He was half German, half Japanese.
His dad was president of a large car firm, and so we used to
cruise around in their cars. It was so much fun. My friends
and I would sneak out at night, and he'd pick us up outside
the gate from where we stayed while working in Japan. We
were not allowed to go anywhere after eight. It was then the
gates would close, and nobody's allowed to leave the prem-
ises. If you do you have to like ask permission'.

'Why?' I asked.

'Because of security reasons,' she said. 'They don't want
you to go missing or have an accident while you're in their
care – it was just the rules. However, we used to sneak out
in our black hooded clothes and like go to town. It was so
much fun, and we'd do it quite often. Yeah, I had sex with
him!'

'With ...?'

'This Japanese guy, who was really nice.'

'What was it like? They say Japanese are different.' It
was a personal question but I was curious.

'Oh it was like a duty. I mean, I remember afterwards
he'd get the box of tissues and, like, clean up afterwards,
you know, like it was a chore. I mean you go ahead and just
do it and then he'd be there mopping up afterwards.'

She laughed.

'No affection?' I asked. 'Nothing?'

'Well, I didn't enjoy it – I thought it was a joke. There was no real passion: it was like just sex where they give you money at the end of it; it felt like a job.'

'Did he pay you?'

'No!'

'Sorry, it's the way you said it. You mean it just felt that way?'

'It felt as if it was a job. There was no foreplay: it was just like right into it. It's [a case of], like, How boring!

'After Japan I went back to Raro.'

Miari stopped her story there (although we'll hear more later). She had promised to go to her parents' home that evening and as it was getting quite late, and decided to make a move. There had been a lot of upset on the island recently, because of a hurricane that had hit another of the Cook Islands, Manihiki, which is in the northern group. Miari's mother was Manihikian, and knew many of the people who died or been lost in the disaster.

When Miari left I couldn't help but think of Kauraka Kauraka, my first connection to the Cook Islands. It was he who, as a civil servant, had invited me to the islands in the late 1980s, after I had written to the government for permission to use one of their uninhabited *motus* (or islets).

It was my first trip to the South Seas. My wife Cathy, who at present was parted from me by a distance of ten thousand miles – and had been for some time – had accompanied me on that first trip, which, as it turned out, was a trial run for the castaway capers she, the kids and I found ourselves involved in. But I'll come back to that in Chapter 3.

I remember my first memory as I walked down the steps of the Air New Zealand plane. Rarotonga smelled of flowers, and I felt physically lighter, as if the cares of home were rising from my shoulders. Waiting for us as we walked through customs was Kauraka Kauraka, a huge man whom Cathy described as a gentle giant. He was wearing a blue shirt and long trousers, and was bare-footed. He seemed to know it was us immediately as he beamed us a smile as large as his physique. Behind Kauraka stood a smiling plump woman in a neat blouse and floral skirt.

'This is my aunt,' he explained. Cathy and I were a little taken aback when they both hugged and kissed us in their natural welcoming way. His English was perfect but his aunt spoke only Maori. He talked the whole time, but all I could think about was the smell of fruit and flowers and the warmth of the air, so sensuous it made my skin tingle. We got into a taxi and were driven past endless ocean on one side and low houses in luxuriant gardens on the other. There were no high buildings, just soft protecting greenery clothing the high mountains inland, and the perfect emptiness of that blue sky over the Pacific.

Soon we arrived at a motel, where Kauraka had paid for our first night's stay. His kindness was unforgettable.

***

I don't know what I'd expected when I saw the name Kauraka Kauraka on the neatly typed letter that arrived at my home in Swansea on that rainy day the previous winter. It had been a dream of mine since childhood, a thirst for travel. I had written to numerous governments within the Pacific. I was in search of an uninhabited island, and Kauraka's letter – which I still cherish to this day – was the most welcoming.

He had been a civil servant then, which was before a recent change of government. He now spent much of his time doing what he loved best: writing, mainly poems and legends of his home island of Manihiki. The day after we arrived, Kauraka took us on a tour of the island; he was waiting on his scooter for us, at the entrance of the motel. He had also borrowed a scooter for us.

We followed Kauraka as he bounced along on his scooter, his red-and-yellow shirt billowing. We bowled along in the warm salt air beside the beach and climbed high into the jungly interior, where fresh water tumbled from high peaks into vegetation as thick as fur. With such variety Rarotonga seemed like a miniature world, isolated in contentment and untouched by history.

Kauraka was a clever man, who loved the islands. The books he had written were in Maori with English translation. 'I wrote a poem to my father,' he said. 'One day I shall read it to you.'

Kauraka taught me a lot about the islands during my visits over the next several years. He never did get to read me that poem – sadly, he died while I was on the islands in

1997, and he was only in his mid-forties. His body was laid to rest on his beloved Manihiki. I'm not sure if I'll ever get to see his last resting place, thanks to Cyclone Martin, which reduced the island to rubble.

2

An Ill Wind

Sir Apenera Short, the Queen's representative in the Cook Islands, received a fax from her Majesty Queen Elizabeth II, from Buckingham Palace, it read:

> I was very sad to learn of the damage caused in the Cook Islands by Cyclone Martin. I should be grateful if you would pass on my heartfelt sympathy to the families of those who have been killed or injured, and my appreciation to all Members of the rescue services.

This was one of the first messages received by the islanders after Cyclone Martin hit the island of Manihiki on 1 November 1997. The island is situated to the north of Raro and has a much smaller population than its sister island – just 700. The effects of Cyclone Martin have been devastating to the population of Manihiki. They lost family, homes and material possessions in one terrible blow, so much so that many are reluctant to return to their islet, looking instead to remain on Rarotonga or shift to greener pastures in New Zealand and Australia. Of those

Manihikians interviewed by Cook Island News, about a third said they would not go back. For them, the horror of the cyclone was too fresh in their minds for them to be able to live on the island again with any peace of mind. They may change their minds in time but many with families on Rarotonga have been urged to settle there, and the signs are that Manihiki will suffer a population loss.

The best way I can bring to you those horrific events and their aftermath is to let some of the survivors speak for themselves.

Matatia Joe's story

Matatia Joe survived Cyclone Martin with his four children and wife. 'That cyclone took everything away from us, all our houses and belongings,' he told me. 'We received the warning around 2 p.m. Saturday afternoon and by 4 p.m. we had started to move away from our house with a few things to get us through the storm.' Once his family were safe, Matatia went to get a rope to tie their house on the *kaoa* or islet. 'I was in the house when a massive wave brought the house down with me in it. I tried to dive under the water to get to the other side and to land. But ended up floating ten metres to a shed that was floating in the water and held on to it – but the iron roof really cut up my right hand.'

He was eventually thrown onto the sand by the waves and, when he turned to look back at their house, found there was nothing there. 'I cried thinking about my family, and then I heard a voice calling out asking if I had seen a baby out at sea but I hadn't. Then I heard another voice calling out: had I seen his daughter, who was missing? And I had to say no again. I was just praying that my family was OK, otherwise I would just give up and die too. I went to look for them and found them safe. They were crying, thinking I was lost, and we all just cried together.'

Matatia says they plan to return to Manihiki. 'We will start everything again and hope for a better living.'

Teretia Piniata's story

Teretia worked for the Cook Islands Pearls Ltd on Manihiki, and the week before the cyclone had been taking a scuba-diving course so she could dive properly.

'On that Saturday we were supposed to go out for another diving lesson when my boss said we couldn't because of the strong winds and high waves,' she told me. Although the island had received a warning, she said they didn't know it would become so bad so quickly. 'It hit the island so fast, I was more amazed at everything than scared, just looking at all the old ones and the children and people crying everywhere. About forty people came to our house to shelter because it's higher ground.' She said they could hear the waves crashing on their home.

'Everyone was crying and praying at the same time. I'm just glad it's all over.' Teretia is willing to go back to Manihiki and get things together and maybe start again, but she said the cyclone would never be forgotten.

Mairi Samson's story

'I worked as a diver for Cook Islands Pearl in Manihiki,' Mairi told me. 'We had prepared ourselves for the cyclone but we didn't expect that Martin would totally destroy everything on the island. All the houses have been flattened down.

'It's still too scary to think about. But I think we will go back and build up our three houses again. My brother and I will go back to Manihiki but we'll send the rest of the family to New Zealand to stay.

'It's a huge loss for us but hopefully we will get things back together – hopefully.'

Barbie Tiati's story

A mother of two, Barbie was in the house when the worst of the cyclone struck. 'I got caught by the high waves inside my house while trying to get some clothes for me and my boys. It felt like the house was squashing the life out of me as the waves came pounding through. I thought that was the end of it.'

Unconscious, she recovered to find herself caught under a concrete block.

'I started to cry for my two boys, wondering whether they were all right, as I didn't know where they were.'

Barbie tried to push the heavy concrete and other things off herself but she couldn't do it: they were too heavy.

'I just kept crying as there was no way someone could find and rescue me because the wind was still blowing and there were high waves.' She called out to the only being who she says could possibly help her. '"Please, Lord, help me," I kept saying.'

At the same time she felt herself trying to push all the rubbish that was holding her down and the concrete lying on her stomach. She freed herself. 'It happened so quickly I knew God had heard my prayer.'

But there was more to come. 'I was trying to get out and a huge wave came and carried me away but I found a *tipani* branch and held onto it.' The branch broke and she grabbed hold of a log until some men saw her struggling in the water and helped her to safety. Barbie was covered with blood but was happy because her boys survived. 'I'm not sure yet whether I want to return to Manihiki or not.'

Tekura Napara's story

'It was the first time I had ever experienced a cyclone disaster in my life,' said Tekura. 'It was very bad: everybody was in a great state of shock and everybody wanted to get off Manihiki.

'There is nothing left for me there now, for me or my family. It's a memory I'll never forget, watching those huge waves hitting everywhere in the village, seeing people drifting away unable to fight the waves and the strong current of the seas.

'No, there's no way I'm going back to Manihiki. It's sad but I just can't bear thinking about the cyclone or returning there.'

Ana Katoa's story

Ana Katoa held onto one of her two children as a wave swept them from safety into the lagoon. 'I lost hold of my daughter and I was in a state of panic, hysteria. I didn't care about myself I was just thinking: Where's my baby?'

But Ana was six months pregnant and still had her other child struggling beside her, so she had to fight on. 'It was human instinct to carry on.'

Her husband Willie managed to get them onto an aluminium boat along with other survivors. But the boat overturned and that was when Ana lost her other daughter.

'We put her in the front of the boat but I think she must have hit the side when it overturned.'

There had been another little girl they had saved in the boat, Ponina, and she also disappeared. A search proved fruitless and Ana and her husband Willie realised they had to save themselves. They held onto the side of the boat for the night, because they couldn't upright it. 'All I could think was I had lost both my children. Willie kept talking to me, worrying about my condition and our unborn baby. I was just praying: "Please God get us through the night."'

Willie started lifting the boat, concerned that the sponge seating underneath might get heavy with water and cause it to sink. 'Out came the little girl Ponina from under the boat. She had survived all that time in a little space. We kept diving underneath to see if our little girl was there as well, but she wasn't.'

It was the next day when they came across a man who had been floating on his back for the entire night. He helped Willie right the boat and they all clambered inside. They ate coconuts to survive, which Willie husked with his teeth. He also made a sail out of a sleeping bag and timber. This eventually got them to Rakahanga, a neighbouring island, from where they were flown to Rarotonga, and Ana learned that the daughter she thought they had lost first on Manihiki had survived.

As for the future: 'I think this will affect the rest of our lives. We lost a life ... but we have to go on. You can't just dwell on the past, you can't: you have to keep on going.'

The cyclone claimed nine lives and to date there are still ten people missing. These were just a few examples of terror, confusion and chaos that gripped the islanders of Manihiki during the cyclone.

The most damaging factor was without a doubt the 33-foot waves that engulfed the island and surrounding *kaoas*. The *kikau* houses, which are houses built on stilts within the lagoon, were swept away with their occupants still inside. The island of Manihiki is inhabited mainly by black-pearl farmers and their families, who have invested time and money in harvesting these precious and rare gems.

I sat on my veranda, looking up at the star-dotted sky, and thought how ironic all this was. The British *Daily Mirror* covered one of the hurricanes that hit the Cooks back in 1993. Two of the staff from the *Mirror* were on Raro at the time: Harry Arnold, the chief reporter, and Harry Page, a photographer. They came to cover a story about me, Cathy and our three young children, Craig, who was then eleven, Matthew, who was seven, and Stacey, who was just four. We had cast ourselves away on a paradise island, and Harry and his editor thought we'd make a good feature.

Little did we know that Hurricane Nisha was to hit our paradise island.

3

In Search of Paradise

The *Mirror* had sent Harry Arnold to see us in our home town of Swansea in West Wales. I had seen his picture in the paper sometimes – a very small picture the size of a postage stamp that they printed in the middle of the page when he did a report. He had a square face and glasses. However, when he stepped out of the station taxi I was not prepared for anyone so opulent. He had a mobile phone, a leather briefcase and a wallet that he flourished at the taxi driver. He was not nearly so intimidating once he got indoors, though. He was friendly, and put his phone and his briefcase on the floor and sat down with me at our low table while Cathy made a cup of tea.

He asked a lot of general questions before he got round to the island on which we were to cast ourselves away. I told him about the people I had contacted on Raro, and how we hoped to go in the next few months.

He asked me the children's ages and what we would live on and whether we would have a boat. He was very interested in the cuttings from the *South Wales Evening Post*.

'So exactly when're you going, Tony?' Harry asked.

'After Christmas I hope,' I said. 'It's the money, see.

We've sold everything so we've nearly got enough, but there's still a bit of saving to do.'

That was an understatement. In my more pessimistic moments I confronted the fact that we needed another £1,000 at the very least. But there was no point in dwelling on the negative aspects: we'd never go if I did that.

'Difficult, is it, financially?'

I told him it was difficult – financially.

He asked me how long we were thinking of staying. What we were taking with us. There were a lot of questions like that. He then went back to London as quickly as he'd arrived.

A day later he was on the phone. 'I think I may have got a deal for you,' he said confidently. 'I think we may be able to get your flights paid for.'

'What?' My voice rose slightly. 'Do you know how much it is?'

'I shouldn't worry about that.'

'It's thousands.'

'It's worth it to the *Mirror* if we can tell your family's story, Tony. We'd want exclusive rights to coverage of the trip, and in return we'd finance your flights and the first few nights' stay on Rarotonga when you get there. Would you be happy with that?'

I caught Cathy's eye. She looked mystified, presumably by the expression on my face.

'I'll think about it,' I said.

'Smile. Big smile, everybody. That's it!'

The *Mirror* photographer - a tall man called Harry Page - had us standing in order along the beach at Mumbles, in order of height: me, then Cathy, then the children. All the kids were wearing the rucksacks we had bought for them, in brutal emerald and magenta and crimson nylon that looked out of place in this light. An icy wind cut into our faces. The sands were brown and ridged and damp underfoot. People leaned over the sea wall to see what was going on.

'I'm freezing,' I said through gritted teeth.

'All together now! Say "cheese"!'

I said it. Several times I said it. We posed while the photographer ran around us, framing our pinched faces in his viewfinder, and getting us all to smile. The children were a lot less distressed by this than I was.

'I think I've got enough,' he said at last, panting slightly. The photographs, when they appeared in the *Mirror*, told the story of how we were leaving Wales for a desert island. But I got that odd feeling of disassociation. I couldn't relate the grinning family in the picture to us, the children bounding up and down the stairs and me and Cathy going to the shops or waiting for the tickets to come through the post.

'It'll all seem real when we get there, Tony,' said Cathy.

I would have thought the same, but the *Mirror* was talking about sending Harry Arnold to join us for a few days.

We went to the doctor's so that we could get vaccinations against tropical diseases. There was a sort of catching of breath when we trooped into the waiting room. Conversation stopped. We occupied most of one wall, and I was aware that people were staring at us. I knew most of them by sight, and they certainly knew us, from the papers. Cathy took the children in one after another. When Matthew came out and Cathy took Stacey in, I caught a glimpse inside the surgery, where a nurse in a white overall stood preparing a syringe. The door closed behind mother and daughter, and almost immediately a great yell went up. It wasn't the nurse and it wasn't Cathy.

'I dowanna go to the island! I dowanna go to the island!'

This was followed by howls of unhappiness, and everybody in the room avoided looking at me. Craig and Matthew nudged each other and grinned. The yelling persisted. People crossed their legs and got up and put their magazines back on the table and blew their noses. I could see they were all formulating a thought about cruelty to children.

At last the door burst open and Stacey shot out, her little face like a beetroot, pulling Cathy by the hand. Cathy was pink too, with embarrassment, and was looking back trying to apologise to the doctor as she was tugged along. We left the waiting room in silence.

My friend Gareth came over on the last day before we left for our flight, to board up the house for us and take us over to his house, where we would spend the night on the floor in their back room. I had borrowed an extra suitcase and, as I put all three cases into the car, I wondered what made them so heavy. I had bought a very expensive book on the life of William Bligh specially, but Cathy had said she'd get something at the airport, so it wasn't books. Gareth had given me a plastic box of fishing hooks and a rod and line. There were saucepans – a nesting set of three for camping that we had got from Millet's – though I couldn't see what we'd wanted three for: we'd have only the one fire. There would be only one tent, too, of the four-person variety.

There were some plastic plates, cutlery, clothes and soap. Craig and Matthew and Stacey had backpacks full of schoolwork and books and toys.

Mr Harris was headmaster to Matthew and Stacey at that point, and he had been very encouraging about their going. 'It's not schooling they'll get when you take them,' he explained. 'But it is education. They'll learn new skills. Different skills. It will all feed into the work they'll be doing when they come back here.' He said it would be a broadening experience, and I found this very encouraging.

Gareth spent most evenings at home drinking beer at his kitchen table, but he gave it a miss the night before we left because he had to get up at five to see us off. The alarm went in pitch-darkness and I got up and peered out between the curtains.

Gareth's house is on high ground, and beyond his back garden Swansea was spread out in a twinkling of street lights, glimmering through teeming rain. A draught knifed through a gap between the window and the wall. I dressed quickly against the cold. While Cathy got the children ready I sat with Gareth at his kitchen table. He gave me a cup of instant coffee and sat down, turning his chair away from the wall. He sat back with his head against a pinned-up drawing his little girl had done at play school, and shut his eyes.

'I remember you coming round our mam's and talking about Canada,' he said. 'We were going to go away and find gold. Do you remember?'

''Course I do.'

I had read about gold-diggers in the library. I thought I would grow up and get out to the gold fields and be rich. As it happened, when we were sixteen, Gareth and I did go away. But we got only as far as Paddington Station in London. I hadn't known London was so big. Gareth used the return half of his train ticket the same night and went home, leaving me in London on my own.

It was strange, contemplating starting a journey across the world from this kitchen, with the kettle on and Gareth sitting there unshaven as if it were a normal day. It would be for him: when we'd gone he'd probably catch up on a bit of sleep, watch telly at lunchtime. It'd be raining here; it'd started already and I could hear it outside. We'd be miles up in the sky this afternoon. And by tonight hurtling over another continent thousands of miles away.

At last we crammed into a taxi that took us to Cardiff for the 7.05 Intercity to Paddington. We got a trolley and trooped onto the platform. There was no train yet, but a lot of people were waiting in the cold. The children had never been on an aeroplane, and they were exited.

We waited with all the early-morning businessmen. There was a loud clearing of the throat on the Tannoy. No London trains would be running, boomed a voice, because of water on the line. Taxis would be provided for passengers who could pick up the 8.15 connection at Bristol Temple Meads.

British Rail apologised.

We struggled into another taxi. It was an ordinary saloon and everybody was squashed, except me in the front passenger seat. We rumbled along the inside lane of a dual carriageway never exceeding forty, and got to Bristol in the rush hour, fifteen minutes late.

The train had gone, said a guard. We could catch the 9.15, take a taxi across London and get the Gatwick shuttle from Victoria. We sped on our way at last, and five minutes out of Paddington the train slowed down and stopped. We stared out of the window for a bit, at the backs of big white houses and other – empty – railway tracks.

'We're going to miss the plane,' Cathy grumbled. She had a watch on; I had sold mine. As I saw it, time had no meaning on a desert island. The children had packed their games away, ready to get off the train. Other people were already standing near the doors, and here we were, stuck. A voice over the Tannoy announced that there was a security alert at Paddington.

British Rail apologised.

Everybody seemed to be listening for something. Another train passing, or a distant explosion. Forty minutes elapsed before the train crawled into the station. London was crowded with high buildings everywhere and roaring with traffic – and I hated it. We got to Gatwick on a packed train with fifty minutes to spare before take-off and dozens of people on the walkways and in the airport.

There was too much to take in at once. The Air New Zealand desk was the only one with nobody queuing at it. Against it leaned a tall man with a camera: it was Harry Page. As I panted up with our trolley he said, 'Let me help you.' He started hauling cases onto the weighing machine, looked round and spoke to me like a conspirator. 'We've got to get through here fast: there's a bloke from the *Sun* looking for you.'

Cathy took our boarding cards from the desk clerk. Harry Page whisked us outside the airport building on a windswept balcony and took our picture. Then he saw us to the departure gate and said goodbye.

'See you in a few weeks.'

'What?'

'Didn't you know? I'm coming out with Harry Arnold.'

'To our island?'

'Yes, isn't that great?'

It might have been great for him, but I hated the idea.

We eventually made it to Aitutaki, with the help of William, a Cook Islands friend we had previously met on Raro. Aitutaki is a volcanic island that has a fringing reef forming a lagoon and atoll. It lies about 200 miles (320 kilometres) from Raro.

Aitutaki has a special sense of magic. It's enormous lagoon boasts clear, turquoise, inviting waters gently stroking bleached shores. Enclosing the lagoon is surf-topped coral reef and a sprinkling of coral islets. Aitutaki's lagoon is about seven and a half miles (twelve kilometres) wide and nine miles (fifteen kilometres) long (north to south). The surrounding waters are a haven to an abundance of fish, including marlin, tuna, wahoo and barracuda. Maina, which was to become our uninhabited island for the foreseeable future (uninhabited apart from us, that is!), lay peacefully within the lagoon, one hour's journey by motor-boat from Aitutaki.

Tere, William's sister, was a widow, and Palmer, their brother, had a family in New Zealand. Here on Aitutaki, Palmer lived in Tere's house.

Tere said she would take us to Maina the same after-noon. We straggled on foot along the gravelly coast road to her house. Palm trees waved above us, and on one side, framed between their trunks, a strip of silver sand sloped into blue water. I remembered our daily walk along

Mumbles sea front to the shops, and suddenly I felt so happy to be here that I'd have paid for Cathy's mum and dad to come out, too, if I'd had the money; I felt sorry for anybody who had never seen this. All this time Cathy had been telling Tere about our journey.

'William said you're ready to go,' Tere said.

'Yes, but we haven't got fishing nets.'

'Palmer will give you those. Junior!'

Junior was Tere's grandson. He came running from the back of the group where he had been walking with Stacey and Matthew.

'Yes, Mama?'

She gave him his instructions. 'And get them some limes and cabin bread.'

'Yes, Mama.'

He loped on ahead to talk to Palmer, whose round figure was rapidly covering the ground ahead of us. Palmer was talking to Craig, and waving his arms, which looked like Indian clubs. His hair was very black, while Tere's was snow-white, and I remembered William telling me that there was a big gap between their ages.

Tere's house, in a garden overhung by trees, had grown organically like coral. It was ramshackle and surrounded by an assortment of ancient, discarded rowing boats, old oil drums and gardening implements abandoned to the jungle. The first few rooms had been erected for Tere as a bride by Richard Marsters, her father, who was a clever carpenter, besides being a missionary. This house of Tere's must have started out as a modest dwelling, and, as Tere's family had become more numerous, first a veranda had been added, then walls were added to the veranda, so that it became a room; and the new room had to have a veranda of its own, which was gradually furnished with table and chairs and hooks on the back wall until sides were added, and it too was on its way to becoming a room.

We set off from Tere's after eating a delicious lunch of chicken and fish, cooked traditionally in an underground oven, in the garden. Then we were off to our island.

We could see part of Maina from the beach near Tere's house: it was a tiny blur further along the coast, about four miles (6.5 kilometres) beyond the wharf at Arutanga. A rowing boat lay upended in the sand. Palmer and Junior and some local boys hauled it onto logs and rolled it down to the water, while Cathy and I and the children stood nervously with our luggage beside Tere. Tere insisted that we must take a bag of limes, to use as an antiseptic, and some cabin bread, the kind that sailors kept in barrels aboard the old sailing ships. Palmer lent us two fishing nets, a machete and a metal container full of water. There was no fresh water on Maina and Stacey had announced that she thought coconut water had a nasty taste and she would not drink it. We were also taking a spear-fishing gun of Junior's, in case he saw dinner on the way. Tere was carrying a vast, brightly coloured umbrella to protect herself from the sun, but I saw her looking at Craig.

'The boy looks a little burned,' she said to Cathy.

'I made him put some sunscreen on this morning, so he should be all right.'

Palmer and Junior heaved an outboard motor onto the boat, and Junior climbed in and shoved it into place as the boys stood in the shallow water, holding the boat steady. When it was still, Tere waded out and climbed aboard, which made it cringe into the water as if a giant forefinger had pushed it down. Palmer helped us all to scramble in with our possessions and waved cheerfully, and the boys gave us a push out into the lagoon. Junior spun the engine and we roared away from the shore – away, it seemed, from Maina.

'We have to zigzag,' explained Tere, seeing my puzzlement and making herself heard over the noise. 'The reefs are very dangerous.'

The water we were crossing was a clear turquoise, paler and greener than the surrounding ocean. Maina is harder to get to than other islets in the Aitutaki atoll because there are treacherous coral reefs close to the surface along the route. Sometimes we sped along quickly, Junior staring intently at the water all the time and not seeming to look where he was going. Then he would suddenly cut the engine and allow us to bob about while he manoeuvred us with an oar over a coral outcrop underwater. Once or twice he had to pivot the engine right out of the water so that the rudder could clear an obstacle near the surface.

Craig and Matthew were trailing their arms in the glistening lagoon and Stacey snoozed happily on Cathy's lap. Junior had just cut the engine again and he turned around, squinting in the sun.

'Big one! You'll need the spear.' Tere shouted.

Junior grabbed the spear-fishing gun from its hooks along the side of the boat and peered into the water. We all saw a long dark shadow in the depths, but it seemed to see us at the same time, and vanished. Junior pulled a face, put the gun back, and ripped the cord of the engine again. Tere sighed, and to divert her I shouted over the noise, 'Your brother told me the weather was bad yesterday.'

'It was! There were big waves only twenty metres out. I thought a storm was coming. But this morning, it was all sunshine again.'

4

Coconuts and Sunburn

Maina was close now. I could see a dusty bank four or five feet high, like a miniature cliff, running along the back of the beach and dividing it from the interior. It was as though the land of the island had been abruptly scraped away by a spade. Behind the beach I saw dense undergrowth out of which thirty or forty tall palm trunks rose at intervals, softly brushing the blue sky. A colony of blackish birds swooped and cried beneath the crowns of the trees. They did not know that they would soon be sharing their home with strangers

It wasn't much easier to erect the tent this time than it had been on that trial run that Cathy and I had made, without the children, a few years before. We had found a good spot, though, in a grassy clearing on top of the bank near the beach, near to where a fallen palm tree grew diagonally from the side of the ridge. It was shaded by a tree with long leaves that stood up from the ground on high, dainty roots like walking fingers.

Cathy stood back and surveyed our new home. She smiled at me and glanced out to sea.

'Look, Matthew, you can just see them still, look.'

Far away in the blue, Junior and Tere, her striped umbrella a little splodge of synthetic colour, zigzagged home. We were going to be alone now, just the five of us. The orange nylon of our tent looked as bright as a traffic cone in the shade under the tree.

'Zip it up, Tony, or we'll get sand flies inside,' Cathy urged.

My legs were itching already. Everywhere you walked these things rose up in clouds.

'I could murder a cup of tea,' Cathy said. 'Keep your shoes on in the water Stacey! Matthew, run and tell her.'

'You're so jumpy,' I said.

'You've got to watch out for them, haven't you? Where's Craig gone?'

'He said he was going to look for coconut husks.'

'Did he have his top on?'

'No.'

'You're a fine example, you are.'

'I'm not burning.'

'You are: your shoulders are all red.'

'They'll be brown by tomorrow. Relax, Cath.'

She shook her head hopelessly at me and went to talk to Stacey and Matthew.

We had picked a good place. Outside the tent a couple of graceful palms framed a sunlit area of sand and water and sky as far as the eye could see. There was silence, except for the rustle of the hot wind and the susurration of the waves against crushed shells. And behind the tent undergrowth too dense to penetrate.

I propped the empty suitcase, which had had the tent in it, against a coconut palm and opened the other one.

There was a cassette recorder with batteries in here, and I was determined to commit our first impressions of the desert island to tape. It was warm when I took it from among the jumble of T-shirts and plastic plates. The sun had penetrated deep inside the case. Already I was so much at one with my surroundings that the cassette recorder seemed the strangest artefact, a hard little black box with efficient-looking buttons, so freakish and unworldly that I wouldn't have been surprised if it had suddenly beamed me up into space. And ripping the cellophane wrapper from a cassette was an unnatural act. I had nowhere to put it. Should I bury it?

'You're sitting right in the fireplace,' said Cathy, dumping a few coconut husks alongside me. 'We need some twigs, Tony. Come on, I'm starving.'

Wherever you go there's pressure.

'It's no good building a fire till we've got some fish to cook,' I said reasonably, and put the recorder back in the suitcase. I left Cathy to find the twigs, while I scrambled down the bank to the lagoon to show Craig how to fish. I crossed a few feet of chalky rubble and twisted driftwood with small lizards and crabs slipping out of my path. The sand near the waterline was crunchy with broken shells and little dry twigs. And then I was on the beach, where the sand was hot, white and silky against the ankles. Stacey came running towards me, holding a small crab by one claw.

'Look, Dad!'

'You can get lots of those, Stace, and we'll use them for fishing with.'

Craig appeared beside me, looking excited.

'I've just been down the shore, Dad. There are some really big crabs along there.'

'We only need little ones for bait.'

'I thought we had to walk out with the nets.'

'Last time,' I said, revealing a plan I had thought up while I was meditating, 'your mum and me used the nets. But we can get bigger fish if we do it another way. We get two big sticks and stick one in the water and one on the sand and run a line between them, with crabs hanging off just under the surface. Then, when the fish bite, we've got them.'

We wandered about near the edge of the beach, looking for sticks that would be long enough. There was quite a lot of dry grey driftwood, and Craig and I soon found one straightish branch each, smooth, silvery, a couple of inches in diameter and taller than a man. I plunged mine into the soft sand at the water's edge and wiggled and plunged it down as deep as I could, which was not very deep. Craig said it was a pity we hadn't brought a spade, but I said the first islanders hadn't had spades, and they'd managed all right.

When the piece of driftwood was steady and vertical in the sand I walked out into the lagoon with the other one, and Craig followed. When I got to waist height in the water he started to swim out, and I passed the branch to him. He had to dive down into the water, which was about six feet (nearly two metres) deep at that point, and plant the stick as I had planted the one on the shore. He did this, after a few tries, and we strung a bit of spare nylon cord that had come with the tent slackly between the two poles so that it hung just above the water. At intervals along the cord I tied strings, and at the end of each one, hanging into the glassy sea, I put a hook with a bit of dismembered crab on it.

'The sun's still hot, isn't it, Cath?'

She had come down to the water's edge and was holding Stacey's hand and paddling.

'There's a lot of sea cucumbers here,' she called. 'We'll have them for supper, shall we? I'm tired of waiting for the fish.' I chose to remain silent rather than reply to Cathy's brand of sarcasm.

But the boys were curious about the sea cucumbers. Craig let go of his pole once he had tied the line on and swam a few strokes inshore. Matthew said eagerly, 'Let's see, Mam.'

Because I was curious I waded over to look at the sea cucumbers too. In the very shallow water there were dozens of them, dotted about singly and clinging to the sand underwater, like slugs after a rainy night. It was their sluglike appearance, black and slimy, that put us off eating them, though William had said they were a great delicacy. I remembered him telling me a Japanese company had wanted to farm them here and air-freight them from the Cook Islands. 'But we would not let them,' he had said, self-righteously. The Cook Islanders, or the Japanese, were welcome to the world's entire supply of sea cucumbers as far as I was concerned. I had trodden on one once, and the insides rolled out red and beige like bloody worms.

'It's what you're used to, I suppose,' he'd said.

I waded back to the line between the poles. Unfortunately once the first strings were tied on and my back was turned, the two poles had lurched gently sideways in opposite directions, pulling the line out of the water. It stretched taut between them, and the strings, with their tempting bait, dangled several feet above the surface. Craig

43

and I tried again, but, whatever we did with those poles, they rocked from side to side and fell over.

'Keep the bait up in the air like that,' said Cathy, 'and you might catch a flying fish.'

She can be so cutting.

Before I had thought of a reply, she said, 'Let's just walk out with the net, Tony, the way we used to.'

'This is a much better way of doing it, if I could get the sticks to stay up, Cath.'

'You can't.'

'Mum, I'm hungry,' said Stacey.

'Look, I can't keep the fire going unless I can stay beside it,' said Cathy impatiently, 'and I can't stay beside it unless you help me do the fishing now. Come on, do it with me. Craig's never done it before, you can teach him tomorrow.'

Reluctantly I let go of my pole and took an end of fishing net from Cathy. Palmer had lent us two nets. One had big holes for catching snapper and other fish in the lagoon, and to use it I needed to be able to swim. Since I couldn't, it stayed in its gauze bag. And there was this one, with smaller holes. It was a big lacy rectangle. One long side had floats on, and we knew from our last island experience that we could weigh it down by tying lumps of coral into the other side.

'Tell us where the shadow is, in the water,' I called to Matthew. From his vantage point on the beach he studied the area near us and pointed to a small shoal of fish. All Cathy and I had to do was approach it carefully, spread the net between us, slap the surface of the water to drive the fish in and walk around in a circle to meet each other.

When we pulled the net up from the sand it was full of little darting silver forms, the size of sprats.

We had eaten our fish, boiled in coconut water over a fire made of twigs and coconut husks, and we were tucking into some pawpaws Craig had found on a tree further inland, when we heard a baby crying. Fear rolled over us like a wave. If I hadn't been so hot I would have shuddered. As it was, we all stopped chewing and sat motionless. Stacey whimpered.

'Shh, Stacey.'

None of us dared move.

After long seconds of staring at each other we heard it again.

A hungry, discontented baby.

There was nobody else here. How could we be hearing this? My eyes flicked towards the machete. William Bligh's stories about cannibal tribes flashed through my mind. Palmer had made a joke about the first Mr Williams on the islands, the missionary priest who came in 1821. All the islanders knew him, and they all, it seemed, knew that he had finished up as a roast dinner, somewhere in Vanuatu. I was sure Palmer had been teasing me, but I wished he hadn't bothered. The cry came again, just behind the tent, followed by a crashing and fluttering – and then the baby wailed far above my head. I jumped to my feet.

'It's a bird. It's all right, it's a bird,' I said, relieved.

'Oh, thank God for that. My heart was pounding,' said Cathy, her hand on her heart and her face white in the gloom.

'Mum, why does that bird sound like a baby?'

'I don't know, Stace.'

'What sort of bird is it?'

'I don't know, sweetheart. Eat up your pawpaw.'

By morning we were still ignorant, but now we knew that there was not just one bird crying like a baby, but hundreds. We had passed a terrible night. Being zipped into a tent with four other people was like being buried alive, but, if you slept out in the dark, clouds of hungry mosquitoes descended on you. Cathy and I lay lengthways and the children slept across the width of the tent and we all smelt strongly of the citronella oil we had smeared on when the sun went down.

I lay on my front because the slightest touch on the toasted flesh of my back felt like a whiplash. Outside, a whole nursery full of babies cried, and heavy forms rustled and clicked and ground across the crushed shells and remains of the fire. My feet were against the zipped-up part of the tent, and outside this inner 'room' was a storage area with no groundsheet. I felt something hard pressing and moving against the canvas and realised that the big coconut crabs were foraging in there. I heard metal grinding against metal as they shoved the nesting pans about, and hoped Stacey would not waken and want to go outside to the toilet because I would have to clear the crabs out before she went through.

I was dozing after hours of discomfort when a rooster cock-a-doodle-doo'd loudly outside.

'Listen to that, Tony.'

'Aagh!' Cathy touched my shoulder and in agony I lurched on to my knees, which was as far as I could go without hitting the roof.

'You hit my sunburn.'

'I only touched you. I'm sorry, love.'

Then Craig piped up. 'Mum, my back hurts.'

'Go on out of the tent, Craig, and I'll have a look.'

I shuffled round, bent double in the orange glow of morning, and unzipped the tent. In the storage area our pans were all tipped over, but I hardly noticed this, because I was so glad to get out into the air.

A large cockerel, which had been prodding at our pile of coconuts, took one look at me and bounded into the undergrowth. Before me I saw the sand, the lagoon and the blue sky, and it was all ours. For a moment I felt the exhilaration that had been missing since we arrived on Rarotonga: the sense of power over my own destiny and delight in a world that seemed made especially for my family and me. Then reality intruded.

'Tony.'

Cathy and Craig had crawled out of the tent behind me.

'Look at Craig's back.'

Craig was crimson all over and big blisters had puffed up on his face and shoulders.

'You're in the same state he is, Tony. I don't think much of that sunscreen.'

'It got washed off, didn't it?'

'You should have kept putting it on.'

'I didn't know, did I?'

One by one the family disappeared into the bushes. I had told them yesterday to cover what they had done by scraping at the earth with a stick, so I hoped they were doing as I had said.

We split up and went looking for pawpaw for breakfast. The fruit swelled in bunches from the trunks of low, pretty trees with a few shady leaves. As the morning went on, the sun grew hotter, and one by one we dozed off in the shade. I had an uneasy feeling; I couldn't have said why.

I woke up because there was a chicken pecking at the ground near me. She was a dirty white colour and when I leaned on an elbow and stared at her she stared right back out of two red eyes. We were both too hot to do much else. The whole island seemed unusually quiet. The water of the lagoon was even flatter than usual, and slid onto the sand like oil.

Something moved near my head. I looked hard at the thin erect roots of the strange tree near the tent and saw nothing at first, and then made out the shape of a lizard, the size of my hand, mottled and wrinkly like an old man's skin. In the ground near me were dimples that I knew concealed hermit crabs. They would come out at night, some were slowly moving near the tent even now. The chicken stabbed the ground with her beak and picked up a small black beetle.

'Tony!'

Cathy's voice made the chicken trot away squawking. My whole family appeared below me on the beach, framed by the coconut palm growing out of the ridge. They were all scarlet. Craig and Cathy were squinting against the sunlight reflected off the beach, trying to see me among the leaves. Matthew and Stacey splashed each other in the water behind them.

I skidded down the embankment.

'We've been looking for eggs,' said Cathy.

'I could do with a nice boiled egg,' I said. 'And soldiers.'

'Fat chance, we couldn't find any. You coming to fish for supper?'

'Let's have some pod with it.'

I set off with Cathy to look for a sprouting coconut. When coconuts fall from the tree and are undisturbed they slowly settle low into the sand and sprout palm leaves from one end. If you pull them up and open the coconut, you find a substance that looks like white candyfloss inside, which you can eat like any other starch. This is known as pod. When you've scooped it all out of the shell, you find coconut oil for putting on your sunburn.

Cathy and I tugged up a couple of coconuts by their leaves and carried them back towards the camp.

'What did you do when I was asleep?' I asked her.

'Craig kept nodding off. His face is an awful mess, Tony. I never knew it was going to be this hot.'

'He should have worn his hat.'

'Yes, well, it's too late now.'

Matthew came running up with a couple of crabs.

'Can we eat these?'

'There's nothing much on them, Math,' said Cathy. She put her pod on the ground and I did the same. Matthew looked disappointed. I said, 'If you boil them in the water with the fish it'll make the fish taste better, won't it, Cath?'

I was willing her to say it would, but, when she replied doubtfully, Matthew pulled a face and put the crabs on the sand.

They shuffled stiffly towards the sea.

'You can help me with the cassette recorder later,' I said to him.

We had our set of three pans for camping, with one

detachable handle. Cathy made the fire with twigs in the middle and coconut husks round the outside because the fibres of the husks burn slowly. She rested the pan of coconut water on the twigs but when they burned low she had to hold the handle with both hands to keep the pan just above the fire, so that the water kept boiling without the whole fire collapsing. The burning twigs made a lot of smoke and Cathy's eyes watered a lot. It was at about this time, with a saucepan full of boiling fish in her hands and smoke in her eyes, that Cathy heard me asking what her impressions of the island were, and asking her to speak up. She was quite rude about the cassette recorder.

She exhibits quite a temper sometimes. She was feeling guilty about the children getting sunburned and I thought she was taking it out on me. So I made no reply.

We didn't sit round the campfire for long that night, because the atmosphere seemed to be in all senses oppressive. Instead, we retired to the tent when the sun went down.

And it was much hotter than last night.

5

Blowin' in the Wind

As soon as daylight came, I would be in control. I pictured myself striding about, taking whatever we wanted, hacking, stripping, building, fishing and digging, converting the island to suit ourselves. But at night the original inhabitants took over. Now, in the silence, I could almost fancy that some great meeting of the animals was taking place on the other side of the island, some big pow-wow about our arrival and the formulation of a plan of campaign.

Yet I knew from my last island experience exactly what was outside the walls of the tent. If I sat up, bent forward and opened the flap of the entrance, if I crawled past the water container and the ashes of the fire and stood upright, the heat of my skin would attract a dense cloud of mosquitoes dancing in the torchlight. And if I beamed the torch down the slope to the beach I would see crowds waving, crowds of hermit crabs packed as close as ruddy-faced trippers on a hot Bank Holiday at Rhyl, nudging and bumping and waving their claws helplessly in the light.

Tonight was quiet. Tonight was different: there was a stillness about it. It wasn't just the choking heat. Not so much as a rustle came from outside. It was too hot to sleep. I took a deep breath, but no air seemed to be drawn into me. The roof of the tent hung three feet above my face and, although my eyes were open, I could see nothing. This tent would not do. We couldn't sleep like this for months on end.

There was a spot where I thought we could build a sleeping hut. I had seen it today, though at a time when Craig was running ahead and I wanted to warn him about something, so I hadn't mentioned it. It overlooked the ocean, where there was more of a breeze and fewer mosquitoes. We could weave a roof out of palm fronds. Cathy had done something like that on our last trip – she made a mat. That was what we would do. We would build a shelter against the sun, with a woven roof, and use it as a school hut in the day. We could make walls. They didn't need much support: with nothing more than a constant breeze, occasional rain and hot sunlight to contend with, the flimsiest house would last for months. Tere had said there'd been no storms for a long time now.

I thought about cutting branches for a shelter with the machete, and felt that I had made a decision. I would start tomorrow.

The machete was outside, stuck into the side of a palm tree.

Nobody else around.

Nobody who could use the machete.

At this moment I was the single conscious human being on this vast blue curve on the surface of the globe.

I dozed ...

'Toneee!'

It was so dark that I didn't know whether my eyes were open or not, but the roar was loud enough to be right inside my head.

'Wha— What is it?'

Cathy's face was close to mine, but it was hard for us to hear each other over the noise. She groped about near my head.

'Aagh! Mind my sunburn.'

She found the torch and switched it on, shielding it with her hand so as not to waken the children.

Black shadows danced over the roof, which bellied down in places, like the underside of a deckchair with a fat lady sitting in it. There was a groaning and shuddering above the roar of the surf, and the guy ropes were creaking and rain was beating a tattoo above us and we could hear the trees wailing and screaming as they bent before the wind.

'Dad.'

'Don't sit up, Craig, you'll hit the tent.'

Matthew woke up and didn't say anything. He lay there rubbing his eyes while his brother looked blearily at me.

'Is it a storm, Dad?'

'Yes, Craig. Don't worry about it. Go back to sleep.'

I don't suppose he was the least bit worried about it.

Craig tried to pillow his ears against his arms to keep out the roar of what we were to come to know as Hurricane Nisha, which was now rising to a howl as the sides of the tent strained upwards from the ground.

Matthew whimpered a little. 'Mammy, I don't like it.'

'It's only a storm,' said Cathy as quietly and reassuringly as was possible over the noise. 'Nothing to worry about. Now don't talk too loud or you'll wake Stacey.'

Cathy switched off the torch and we lay on our fronts beneath the low-slung canvas, not speaking above the tumult. You'd have had more space at the coalface. I pressed my chest against the groundsheet, trying to extend as much of myself as I could along the ground to keep the tent from lifting up. The gale was trying to dislodge it, to prise it from its moorings as carelessly as my fingernail had flicked a thorn from my leg this afternoon. I had heard of islands disappearing in hurricanes. Everything above the waterline – trees, living things – just torn away and flung into oblivion by the cruel wind.

Under the groundsheet I could feel movement. Rainwater was filling up the sand. With horror I imagined the island simply collapsing inwards, subsiding into the sea.

I struggled to turn over, supporting myself on my elbows.

'Watch out, you'll get water in.'

'Sorry. How long has it been like this?'

'I've been awake hours. I heard the suitcases go.'

I could hear them myself. It sounded as if somebody was banging doors. There was a mad poltergeist out there, flinging suitcases, pots and pans, the water container, the T-shirts, which had hung motionless in the sunset from the bark of a coconut palm – tossing all this across the beach, battering the hermit crabs, pushing at the trees, trying to uproot us. I thought of the machete. Then I pretended I hadn't thought of it. I preferred not to. I had never wanted to be the target in a knife-throwing act.

I had heard stories. There was no reason to think that this violence was being suffered anywhere else. It was like a judgement: we had only just arrived, and the elements were directing their power at us in a way I could never have foreseen. A bolt from the blue: I had heard the phrase. A thunderbolt. What was that? Perhaps the spirit of the place had risen up and was out to get us. Perhaps Tangaroa, one of the great gods of the Polynesian pantheon. Kauraka had told me how the Reverend Williams had destroyed images of the god, probably depleting his *mana* or sacred supernatural power. Maybe this was Tangaroa's revenge. Perhaps the god had been mortally offended by having a Williams on Maina. And the other living creatures had deserted us and left us to weather the storm alone.

I felt a pang of guilt. Thanks to me, Cathy and the children were in danger. A suspicion that I had never admitted to before wormed its way to the surface. What if they had come not because they wanted to, but because they didn't want to disappoint me? What if this was all a charade, to humour me in my stupid overconfidence?

'It'll pass,' said Cathy. 'We're fine here.'

I dragged my mind back to reality. 'Is that the lagoon?'

'That's the roaring, isn't it?'

'Yes. Do you think it sounds too close?'

I could hear layers of sound, pick them out, and interpret the thundering soundtrack that was running outside. I had never seen waves in the lagoon, yet there was a rumble, a crash, high on the beach. Too close. But what bothered me more was the constant thudding and banging.

'There's coconuts falling all over,' I said.

'It's a bit late to worry about that,' said Cathy. 'There isn't anywhere else to shelter.'

Her fingers linked with mine and we lay still amid the uproar.

Craig and Matthew were awake. I thought it better I didn't show that I was getting worried.

I kept thinking it would go away but it didn't. The storm seemed to rage for hours. At last the rain slackened, and I saw a twinkle of grey light where the zip of the tent ended.

'I'm going out,' I announced.

I crawled through the opening and was still on all fours when I saw why we should move. The scene before me bore hardly any resemblance to the paradise of yesterday: the fine white sand was beige and wet; the sky yawned grey as a Swansea sky; the arching, straining palms were a dismal monochrome; coconuts bounced furiously across what was left of the beach; and, most terrifying of all, the sea was black and vicious and hurtling forward waves as high as a man. It rolled up and spent itself against a coconut palm only six feet away. I turned, still on my knees, to go back into the tent, and the gale seemed to take me by the shoulders. Somehow I scrambled back inside in an eddy of leaves and dust.

'We must move.'

Cathy must have seen the alarm in my face, but she knew better than to frighten the children. Craig and Matthew were sitting up, hugging their knees like elves and shivering now under the sides of the tent.

'All right, you boys, now pack up everything you can into your rucksacks.'

We hunched in the gloom with our legs stretched out in front and scrabbled around Stacey, who was dozing floppily with her thumb in her mouth. I shoved things into bags. Bright little messages flashed by:

DURACELL: FOR LONGER LIFE

RAROTONGA: THE LAST PARADISE

Cathy seized the brown paper bag of cabin bread that Tere had given us.

'We'll have to go into the interior,' I said, trying not to sound too melodramatic.

It had been a joke before: 'the interior'. It sounded like an expedition to the source of the Amazon. But I had to get them away from that wall of black water.

'Is the sea coming up?' Cathy asked.

'It's very close,' I said.

It was too close. I thought of Stacey, and the wind out there.

'She won't be able to stand up in it, Cath.'

'I can hold her.'

Stacey was waking up now. Her mother pushed her hair out of her eyes.

'Come on, sweetheart, we've got to go now.'

She was half asleep. I could see she would have to be dragged from the tent or she would lapse back into a doze. She was so small, lighter probably than the suitcase with the cassette recorder and batteries in it that had been lifted and hurled against a tree. I thought how difficult it had been for me to move into the wind.

'I think we have to stop the children getting blown away. We have to tie them to something.'

The others were following me as I hauled myself out into the storm. There was water in the wind – whether rain or sea spray I couldn't tell – and as I stood up I could see the deep pools of water that swung across hollows in the tent canvas. Cathy staggered and grabbed my arm, as she stood upright.

'Can you hold Stacey?' I shouted. I didn't wait for an answer. 'She might get swept away.' I needed rope to lash Stacey down with, and there was one within sight, but it needed cutting. As I turned towards the place where the machete had been, the wind took me and I hurtled towards it as if frogmarched at great speed. The machete was still wedged in the tree. I jerked it out and strained double on my way back to the tent. The others were on their way now, all holding hands, bending into the wind, plodding bravely along the top of the beach. Cathy was struggling to carry a suitcase and keep tight hold of Stacey's hand as she led the children a little way along the edge of the under-growth. At that point there was a gap between two bushes where you could pass through to the interior.

They left me ten yards behind them. I was hacking at the guy ropes with my machete. Rain lashed into my eyes and the salt spray smacked the trunks of the coconut palms. I tugged pegs out of the ground. Once it was released from the ropes' tension, the tent collapsed under the weight of water. It was so heavy and sodden that it didn't immediately fly away. I couldn't lift it. Instead I battled to roll it up, dragged it behind me, clutched the long ropes that I had cut from it and staggered after the others.

I caught up with them in a stony clearing between trees. We were all gasping from the struggle against the wind. I dropped the end of the tent that I had been hauling.

'Come over here, Stacey,' I shouted. She let go of Cathy's hand and took mine.

'Hug the tree for a minute,' I yelled. I got down on my knees as she obeyed, stretching her little arms around the hairy trunk of the coconut palm. It was when I passed the tent rope under her armpits that she turned around and I saw a stricken look in her eyes before the wind blew her hair over her face. She let out a yell: 'Mammy!' It was a yell you hear right across the playground when somebody else's four-year-old is being bullied at going-home time.

'Mammy, I dowanna be tied, I dowanna, he's tying me –'

She wriggled furiously. She wouldn't keep still. I was struggling to hold the machete with my foot to stop it from skittering away in the wind, and the tree was groaning back and forth like a drunken old sailor while I tried to tie a proper knot in the rope. I was no match for Stacey. She got away and clambered into her mother's arms with a tear-stained face.

'It seemed like the best idea,' I muttered.

For the rest of the morning we huddled in the clearing. There was whitish rubble underfoot and above us sixty-foot coconut palms swayed so forcefully that the ground beneath us seemed to heave and roll with them. I had no sense that we were on dry land. I felt as if we were on board a flimsy ship amid a raging ocean.

Heavy rain began again and we fought to put up the tent. I tied some of the ropes around trees and kept the rest anchored with some big stones. We crawled inside with all we managed to save from the beach, and sat, breathing the foul scorched scent of each other's skin.

Breakfast was flying about in the sea and wind outside, and I wasn't eager to risk hunting it. The cabin bread didn't look like breakfast. It was like thick dry slabs of cardboard. After a few hours of playing 'I Spy' and answering questions like 'Why is the wind so loud, Dad?' we fished it out of Cathy's bag and ate it. It tasted like a sample left behind by Captain Cook. But it staved off the hunger, and we sucked limes that Matthew had stuffed into his rucksack in the flight from the tent.

As the day wore on the sun emerged, the sea grew calmer, and the wind died down. We went out. The island looked littered and wrecked, like a dustbin overturned by stray dogs. Tomorrow we would build a shelter. Tonight would be our last in the tent. I would rather lose all the blood in my body to mosquitoes than spend another night in that inferno.

Nothing happens quickly on the island. The next day, a calm and sunny one, was well advanced, and we had barely made a start on the shelter, when I saw a speck bobbing across the lagoon from the direction of Aitutaki. I was fishing at the time, with the small net. Cathy was up to her waist in the lagoon, washing clothes, which the children had picked up from all over the beach after the storm. The children were near the camp, playing. The sun was past its height and, had the beach not been littered with debris, smashed shells, driftwood and broken branches, this would have been an idyllic scene.

I hauled the net onto the sand. Then I turned to stare at whatever it was that I had seen. A boat, certainly. The men from the *Mirror* might turn up at any time, but we were unlikely to see them so soon. I was dreading their arrival: they would want something from me, and I was not quite sure what it was.

I comforted myself that it was most likely just Tere and

Junior in the boat, coming to see how we were after last night's storm. Well, they would see that we had been through it and survived. I looked proudly at my catch: fresh silvery little fishes gleaming in the evening sun. They would be delicious cooked in coconut water with a squeeze of lime. There would be plenty for everybody.

I made a space clear of fallen branches and sodden driftwood, sat on the beach in the sunset and began to clean the fish. I grew engrossed in what I was doing. Practical tasks like this are therapeutic. You learn to do them efficiently and it frees your mind for other things. I was thinking about Bligh and the *Bounty*, my thick book with a stiff grey cover, which had blown into the lagoon and had hurled back to shore on a wave. It was the only book I had and I dearly hoped it would dry out all right. Some of the children's schoolbooks had been ruined by the water.

I looked out to sea. The boat wasn't coming in a straight line, because of the reefs, but I thought I could see three or four figures in it. I would look again when they got closer. Above the soft slapping of the waves, I could just hear the children and an occasional interjected word from Cathy.

Sitting here gutting fish with my fingers, I was attracting thousands of sand flies. I could feel sharp shells pressing painfully into the skin on the backs of my legs, and I shifted, sending the cloud of tiny flies high into the air for a moment. I stood up, scraping sand from my legs, and looked out to sea again. Two white blobs and two dark ones sat in the boat.

The storm had been very stressful and we had had little sleep since we came to the island. The sun was now warm, pleasantly warm, on my face. I lay down for a moment, shielding my eyes with my arm.

Cathy woke me up. 'Look!'

Tere and Junior had stopped the boat's engine and the craft sat calm on the lagoon. A pink figure in tight denim shorts, with his back to me, was struggling over the side, gingerly holding a pair of sandals high above the water. Another man, much taller, was standing up and wobbling against the horizon.

'It's Harry and the other Harry.'

The two figures, the tall and the short, both wearing large brimmed sun-hats with fringed straw edges, waded towards us. Cathy and I waved to Tere. We stood at the edge of the lagoon like a welcoming committee, the Mayor and Lady Mayoress of Swansea on their best behaviour for the arrival of royalty. Under their hats Harry Arnold and Harry Page looked earnest. Their skin was burned scarlet by the sun but you could see white flesh where their shirtsleeves began. They were both sweating. They stumbled through the last few feet of clear water.

'Ow,' muttered Harry Arnold. Harry Page made a hissing noise behind his teeth. The shells are quite sharp underfoot if you're not used to them. I said, 'You found us all right, then.'

Harry Page looked at me as if I were mad. As for Harry Arnold, the Savile Row look that had seemed so out of place on our front step had been left far behind. I wished the neighbours could have seen him this time. He had a sort of cutlass stuck into his belt. He said, ''Scuse the shorts.' He mumbled something about his honeymoon and the shorts having spent twenty years in a cupboard.

The children lined up behind us. Cathy and Tere began

a shouted conversation across the water. Harry Arnold, wincing a bit on the sharp shells, trod cautiously up the beach with me and the children. His sandals were made of a very thin plastic. I guessed he had bought them in Tahiti. Glancing behind me, I could see Cathy looking mortified, like when somebody comes round and she's sorting washing all over the kitchen floor.

Harry Arnold stopped, shifting his cutlass slightly, and stared in dismay at the torn foliage and broken wood. He must have thought it always looked like that.

'Were you aware of the cyclone at all?' he asked.

The island seemed crowded. Just four more people, and it was uproar. The beach felt like Minehead. Everywhere you looked there was somebody.

Harry Arnold followed me towards the shady patch by the tent, warily clutching the knife on his belt. Harry Page unslung a camera and a pair of sandals from his neck, left them in a heap on the beach and walked away from all of us. He looked a bit greenish under his hat, I thought, not at all the cheery character we had met at Gatwick.

'The sea doesn't agree with him,' said Harry Arnold, who had a hunted look and kept sneaking glances over his shoulder. He was conscious of Tere behind him. She had stepped majestically onto the shore, holding her umbrella aloft, and was scrutinising the two Harrys from a distance. Harry Page marched alongside the lagoon.

'Big Harry! Don't go into the water without your sandals!' Tere scolded. The tall fellow hesitated and stopped. Tere scanned the beach for Junior, who had jumped out of the boat and was pulling it ashore.

'Junior! Give me my bag from under the seat there.'

Junior heaved a huge laundry bag across the water to

her. She subsided onto the sand with it and began rummaging. Cathy sat down to talk with her.

At the clearing outside the tent I sat on the ground. Harry Arnold did the same. Then he noticed a crab shooting into its hole and got up.

'I never thought you'd come this quick,' I said, as he selected a new position and hesitantly sat down again. I was at a bit of a loss. Now that he was here, there seemed to be no social emollient to smooth the path, somehow. No coffee or tea to offer and not a lot of point in asking how they had got here. He explained that anyway.

'We got the inter-island flight to Aitutaki yesterday afternoon. This is just a recce, just a brief visit to find how the land lies. We'll do the pictures and interview tomorrow and the next day ...' Harry was peering at me with a horrified look. 'You seem a bit rough, if you don't mind me saying so. What's happened to your back? And your face?'

'Sunburn.'

'The children are burned as well. Didn't you bring any sunscreen?'

When I explained that we had not expected such intense sunshine, he looked unimpressed.

'Well maybe you'd better wear a T-shirt for the photographs.' The children came running up from the beach with Cathy walking behind them, smiling.

'Tere's gone to sleep on a coconut,' Craig said. I could see Tere's form, as she lay on her side near the waterline. Her head was indeed resting on a coconut. The devoted Junior was sitting beside her, gently waving a palm-frond fan.

'She's asleep, is she?' asked Harry hopefully. 'Does she go to sleep often?'

'She goes to sleep when she's eaten her spaghetti,' Matthew explained, as though he were giving guidance to the habits of some rare wild creature. 'She's got cans of spaghetti and corned beef in her bag.'

'Reminds me of Queen Salote,' murmured Harry. 'Dynamic woman, isn't she?'

'She's very good-hearted and kind,' I told him. 'It's her brother who's William Richard in Rarotonga, that I told you about, you know. They're the third generation since William Marsters, who came from Gloucestershire in the last —'

'Yes, I believe you did tell me. Is this where you sleep? Where do the children sleep?'

He struggled to his feet as I showed him the tent. He didn't say much. In fact he had an air of disbelief.

'Just the one tent?'

I explained that we had wanted to burden ourselves with as little luggage as possible. I told him how we had made a start on the hut. Harry Page emerged from the bushes and muttered something about failing light. They prepared to leave.

'We'll be back tomorrow,' they promised. Harry Arnold said Tere had told them it was important to return to Aitutaki in daylight so that the reefs were visible underwater. He also said he'd be bringing us a surprise on their return. They set off, looking grave, I thought.

'I told him I wished they'd waited a bit before they came,' I said to Cathy, as we strolled down to the waterside to collect the fish I had caught before the boat landed. 'The place does look in a terrible state, doesn't it?'

'I hope they don't think it's always like this,' Cathy

said. 'By the way, I told Harry Page he could take pictures of us putting the hut up tomorrow.'

But I was not to be distracted. The visit had made me uneasy. 'Suppose your dad sees Craig's blisters in the newspaper,' I said. 'He'll be on the next flight, Cath.'

My father-in-law had once threatened to come out and fetch us if he thought anything was wrong. The idea that he might have meant it made me dread the day the *Mirror* printed our pictures. I could see the headline now: MAN RISKS FAMILY'S LIVES ON DESERT ISLAND. And Cathy's dad, his face puce, marching across the hot tarmac at Rarotonga Airport for a confrontation. I hate confrontation.

Cathy took my hand. She kissed it; it was the only bit of me that she could kiss: the rest was too sunburned.

'I wouldn't worry. If Dad ever did come it'd probably mellow him out a bit.'

6

Cassettes and Cameras and Cans of Lager

We had not long finished our breakfast next morning when Tere's boat again appeared on the horizon.

Cathy swore under her breath. 'Help us get the washing-up done, Stacey. Matthew, go and tidy up the tent. Craig, shift some of those coconuts, will you? They're all over the place.'

Cathy and Stacey were just finishing washing up in the lagoon when the boat came within shouting distance. I walked across the sand to meet it. I strode into the water, smiling. Everyone on board was yelling at me. After a while I understood that Tere and Harry Arnold were asking me to grab the front of the boat and pull it into shore. Cathy had followed. She turned away in embarrassment when she saw that Harry Arnold had got a video camera on his shoulder, and he was taking our picture as we tugged the boat in.

Harry Page took no notice of what the other Harry was doing. He swung out of the boat with a lot of camera equipment, muttered a greeting, and tramped past me up the beach. His face was shaded by the fringed edges of his hat brim.

'The other Harry's taking video pictures, is he?' I enquired as he sloshed by. 'What's that for?'

'Plans for you,' he grinned. 'Big plans for you. Career in television.' He unslung his gear onto the sand, squatted beside it and started fiddling with lenses and light meters. A crab waddled away at the sound of Velcro ripping.

This time Cathy helped Junior to heave Tere's bag off the boat.

'I shall wait for them again,' Tere announced, up to her ankles in the water of the lagoon. 'The Harrys are going to work for several hours, they tell me. Junior, fetch me two coconuts.'

Tere created a little force field of energy wherever she walked. As soon as she looked at you, you felt you should be doing something. She strode up the beach to the place where our low coconut palm grew diagonally from the ridge, and sat in its shade. She settled herself into the sand with grace, straight-backed and cross-legged, closed her eyes and waited for Junior to bring her the biggest green coconuts he could find. I could see him in the background, shinning up a tree. She opened her eyes.

'Little Harry!'

Harry Arnold was gingerly exploring the spot where I had been fishing yesterday and he pretended not to hear her. The sand was hot and damp and he was paddling, carrying his sandals.

'Don't go into the water without your shoes!'

Approaching him, I saw that he had got that hunted look again.

'What's all this palaver about shoes?' he asked in a quiet voice as if Tere, who was fifty yards away, might hear.

'There are stone fish,' I explained. 'They lie in shallow water and they've got spikes. If you trod on one accidentally it'd be fatal.'

He quickly shoved his feet into the plastic sandals and tried to look composed.

It was a very warm day already, though the sun hadn't been up more than three or four hours, and I could see that perspiration stood in beads on his forehead.

'Interview first,' he said. We strolled back to the tent where Cathy, the children and I, knowing that visitors were expected, had tried to collect those of our possessions that had been damaged by the storm, and pile them neatly alongside our suitcases. The heat of the sun beat through my T-shirt to my back, making the blisters ache. There was quite a strong breeze, but it felt about the same temperature as a car exhaust. Harry Arnold sat down with all of us. Harry Page prowled around the edges of the group, taking pictures.

'Don't mind me. Just ignore me.'

Craig, Matthew and Stacey found this easy to do. It was as if the most natural thing in the world were to be drinking from a coconut in the mid-Pacific, with some fellow from Surrey in a floppy hat crawling out of the undergrowth with a camera to take your likeness every second gulp.

'The children are very adaptable,' I said to Harry Arnold.

'They need to be. Oh, by the way, I told you I'd bring a surprise.'

He jumped up and ran down to the boat. Harry Page took more pictures; I felt a complete fool. I wanted Tere to be in the picture but apparently her being present would ruin the story. The other Harry returned carrying a large plastic bucket that looked heavy. It turned out to be full of crushed ice. Nestling in the middle were tubs of ice cream, one for each of us, and milkshakes for the children, whose eyes shone. There were cans of lager for the grown-ups. I tugged off the ring-pull and thanked him, though I never drank lager normally.

I got that sense once again that I was touching an arte-fact from an alien planet. I would have liked to explain this: that cassettes and cameras and cans of lager belonged to another world, that they were invaders, and that on this island I could drop out of the century and the culture into which I had been born. This was the point: here, on the island, there was no sense of the twentieth century. But somehow when I said all this it didn't seem to impress him with the same force that it had me.

He was concerned about our distance from medical assistance, he said. With Cathy being an epileptic. Did we have the flares the *Mirror* had provided? I had brought them in one of our suitcases, though it seemed highly unlikely to me that, of the thousand people who live on Aitutaki, one of them would happen to be awake at night at exactly the minute when one of our flares shot across the sky, if it ever did. I had no idea how to use them, and in any case those flares repelled me. I didn't want to have them with me. They signified mistrust of the island. I felt no mistrust, especially now, since the storm was over and

I thought that we had survived the worst that could happen.

So I would have liked to throw the flares into the sea and not drink the lager, but I was too polite.

I told him about the Marsters family, and urged him to interview Tere and Junior, but he said the story was about us, not them. He seemed more interested in the risks he thought we were taking.

I said, 'When I was small my parents had us up in the Valleys. There was no telephone and it was a long way for an ambulance, so how can you think this is any worse?'

Remoteness is more than just distance. I would have liked to explain this. You can be isolated anywhere.

'There's a good lad,' Harry Page told Craig from behind his lens, the motor drive whirring obediently.

Harry Arnold had stretched his hand up the trunk of the coconut palm to provide support for one of Craig's feet. He had shoved my son as high up a coconut palm as he could reach, and Craig was clinging on desperately while at the same time turning and grinning down at the camera.

'He hasn't learned to climb them yet,' I muttered, for about the fifth time.

Harry Page trod on my foot and swore under his breath, and I dodged sideways. 'Harry,' he said to his friend, 'give the boy the coconut.'

'Got it?' said Harry Arnold through his teeth, holding the coconut above his head. Craig let go of the trunk with one hand and wobbled down and grasped the coconut to his chest. He never stopped smiling.

'Stay right there. That's great. Smile. That's excellent. Keep smiling. Get your hand out, Harry.'

I stood at his shoulder and said, 'If his sunburn shows I don't want that in the paper. It'll upset the relatives.'

'Yup, yup,' he muttered, stooping to get an angle on Craig, who was stoically grinning as he clung to the tree with his feet and clasped the coconut in his arm.

When Harry Page had got enough shots of Craig up the tree, he beckoned Cathy over.

'Washing shots, dear,' he said, like a conspirator. 'If you could get a few clothes together and wash them in the lagoon for me, there's a good girl.'

He wandered about snapping the vegetation while Cathy hurried to collect some T-shirts from where they had been drying on a branch.

Harry Arnold was making some adjustment to the video camera and he said, 'You could show me where this hut is that you're building, Tony, if you would. Then maybe when Harry's finished with Cathy you could both do a bit more building for the video.'

'It's over there.' I had taken a couple of steps when I heard a choking cry from above. The green coconut banged heavily to the ground and Craig shot down the trunk after it with a suppressed squeal. His face was red and so were the insides of his legs.

'God, sorry, Craig,' said Harry Page, evidently concerned. 'Completely forgot you were up there.'

Craig hobbled after us to the hut. Stacey took his hand and Matthew followed, carrying half a dozen of his figure men. These were models about four inches high, which represented various soldiers, Terminators (as seen in Schwarzenegger movies), Viking raiders and fierce creatures from space. Since we had rescued the figures after the storm he took them with him everywhere, and was quite likely to slope off at any moment and enact a short drama with them, murmuring to himself in the voices he had given to their different characters.

The storm had made a clearing a few hundred yards from our tent, overhung by a couple of low palm trees. We had begun to stake out a four-sided hut in this space, using the palm trees as one gable end and two tall sticks in the ground as the other. The walls would be made by sticking palm fronds into the ground.

Harry Arnold saw what we had done. 'Oh, it's quite straightforward, isn't it? You don't need to weave them together or anything.'

'That's right, and you make the roof the same way.'

I went off with Craig and Matthew to find some more palm fronds and saw Cathy up to her waist in the lagoon with a bar of soap and some brightly coloured washing under the noonday sun. Harry Page stole along the shore in his hat, snapping shot after shot. 'We usually sleep at this time,' I said, approaching him across the sand. He said something about having a day's work to do and asked me to walk towards him with the children and some palm fronds. The white sand reflected blistered heat onto our faces as we dragged the fronds towards him and Harry Arnold, who had now got his video camera on his shoulder and was busy directing us from the bushes.

'Right, if you could all do that again from the top.

Come in from right of the frame – that's it. *Smile*, please, Tony.' Obediently we trailed our fronds towards the hut again. I thought it was stupid to keep smiling: it's not what you do on a desert island. Cathy came to join us. I wished that I were lying down in the shade. Harry Arnold stole forward in his little shorts with his purposeful knife in his belt and the video camera on his shoulder.

'Get your arse out of my picture, Harry,' growled Harry Page.

'Whose story is this, anyway?'

'Christ knows, but you're not supposed to be in the shot, mate.'

We stood around while they argued and then Harry Arnold said, 'What I want you to do, Tony, if you wouldn't mind, is say a few words to the camera.'

'There you are, Tony, you're going to be a film star,' said Cathy cosily.

'What words? What's this for?'

'Promotion. Sunday night in the middle of *Poirot*. All we need is something like, "I've come ten thousand miles with my family to live on this deserted island and you can read why I did it in tomorrow's *Daily Mirror*."'

I positioned myself where he told me to, and when he said 'Action' I began.

'I've come ten thousand miles to live on this deserted island and you can read all about it in the *Daily Mirror*. That wasn't right, was it?'

'I'll write it down for you.'

He tore off some pages from his shorthand pad, wrote the sentence in big letters and got Harry Page to stand beside him, holding them up.

'All right, action.'

'There's something moving beside your foot, Harry,' said Harry Page, and Harry Arnold jumped in the air with his video camera.

'It's only a crab.' Stacey solemnly removed it. They settled down again.

'Action!'

I peered into the unfriendly black lens.

'I've come ten thousand miles with my family to live on this deserted island and you can read why I did it in tomorrow's *Daily Mirror*.'

'And again, and put the stress on "with my family".'

I did it again.

Then I did it again, saying 'desert island' instead of 'deserted island'. All three of the children were squatting on the ground, watching me. A chicken was pecking the ground behind the two men from the *Mirror*. They shifted out of the sun a bit.

'You don't look very cheerful,' said Harry Page, when I had recited the sentence at the lens for the eighth time.

'It's so unnatural,' I said, squirming. 'What do I want to say this for. I don't want to talk to millions of people.' Harry Page sighed and said something about the meaning of life. Harry Arnold said they'd got enough and thanked us very much. Cathy offered them a drink of coconut water back at the tent and I went to find Tere and Junior.

I felt embarrassed; I wanted the Harrys to go. They made too many demands; they brought pressure with them, I thought. I would have explained this to Tere, but she had woken up and was setting out her afternoon tea:

three coconuts and two cans of corned beef. She had drunk the few litres of sweet water from inside her coconuts and was now busy opening the cans with a knife. Cupping her hand, she scooped some soft white flesh from inside a coconut, wrapped a thick slab of corned beef in it and tucked in, as you would with a sandwich. Tere and I sat together in the shade while the others gathered at the tent behind us.

7

The King of the Island

In the far distance across the lagoon, away from Aitutaki,
I could see shadows that were other islands. I had heard
that tourist boats went from Aitutaki to One Foot Island.

'Why's it called One Foot Island?' I asked Tere.

She swallowed a mouthful of corned beef and told a
story she had told many times before.

'Once upon a time a man and his son landed there. But
a hostile war party had followed them from another island.
The man said to his son, "Walk quickly to that palm tree
and climb right up to the top and stay there." The son
obeyed, and once he was safe and invisible up the tree the
father followed. He placed his feet very carefully in the
footprints the boy had left in the sand. Only he went right
past the tree, so that his own prints continued; and when
the war party arrived, they saw the prints and thought that
there was only one person there. They followed the tracks,
caught the man and killed him, but the boy up the tree
they didn't find. That is why it's called One Foot Island.'

She munched steadily through her supplies while
Junior slept a few feet away. Suddenly she said, 'Do you
know why there are no dogs on Aitutaki?'

I hadn't noticed that there weren't any.

'No.'

'Because there used to be leprosy. Do you see the little *motu* this side of One Foot Island?' She pointed at a shadow across the water. 'That was once a leper colony. Until the 1960s it was. And people thought that dogs carried the disease, so we don't have any dogs to this day.'

I thought of being isolated as a leper, and the idea chilled my heart. It was one thing rejecting the world, but quite another to be rejected by it.

The Harrys were gathering up their cameras and slipping and sliding down the bank to the beach with them. Harry Page landed near us in a shower of sand.

'Most beautiful light I've ever had,' he said, adding sadly, 'We'll be back in London on Thursday.'

'Do you think you got what you wanted?'

'Oh, I think so. It'll make a great story.'

Harry Arnold came down with his video camera. He was carrying a big piece of white coral. There was lots of it on the beach since the storm.

'I think I'll take this home. You'd pay fifty pounds in Harrods for a piece this size,' he said.

We said our goodbyes to the two Harrys, and they were gone as quickly as they had arrived.

I woke up every morning for days feeling relieved that the men from the *Mirror* had been and gone. I hadn't realised how much the prospect of their visit had been weighing on my mind. But now that we had discharged our obligation I was worried in case Cathy's father took on at the sight of the pictures. We were still suffering physically. The blisters on my face and back were septic and oozing, and Cathy and the children were covered in red bumps from mosquito bites.

The tent seemed more like a hot coffin every time we had to get into it, yet the hut we had made was no protection against mosquitoes at night. So to put off zipping ourselves into the tent we talked and sang around the camp fire for hours after dark. Coconut husks smouldered like twisted vermilion tongues and cast a glow upwards to our faces, accentuating the eye sockets. Crabs shuffled briskly through the undergrowth outside our circle of light, or shouldered their way up from the sand near the fire. Sometimes the baby-cry birds whimpered. Stacey spotted mosquitoes like a cat, and jumped up and smacked her hands together when she saw one, bursting the insect in a gobbet of blood.

Beyond our little group the sea lay black and so did the islands, uneven humps on the horizon. The sky seemed miles higher than in Wales. It was full of stars, great trails of glittering dust, and some that twinkled very big and white like the ones on a Christmas card.

Junior had told me that there are no street lights on Aitutaki at night. I thought of him stumbling home from the village by torchlight along the gravel road, no dogs barking, just the rustle of the surf and the wind through the palm tops.

Cathy and the children had slowed down. I noticed especially how Craig had relaxed, having been so tense at school with all the homework. Sitting round the campfire, we heard about Craig and Matthew's friends and school-teachers in a way we had never done when we lived in

Swansea. The boys would not normally have told us which teachers could keep order and which children bullied the others and who got punished for what. Especially since Craig started at senior school, we had heard none of this, because, although we could go to parents' evenings and find out how well he was doing in history or maths, like other parents, we saw only the public face of school. Now, ten thousand miles from the spring term, we heard what it was really like. A tapestry of intrigue and politics, it was. Boyfriends and girlfriends. Children of ten going out with each other. Cathy and I were careful not to laugh.

Matthew was scornful. He said girls were sissy. Craig did not seem so sure. He asked me whether I had had a girlfriend when I first went to comprehensive. I told him I had, but there was plenty of time to think of girls.

'D'you think there's treasure on this island, Dad?' Craig asked me one night. The flickering embers of the fire illuminated his elfin face, his eyes agog with curiosity under his yellow fringe.

'They say there's treasure on Suwarrow,' I told him.

'Last time we were here. William told us there used to be treasure on Palmerston [one of the northern islands],' Cathy remembered. 'His grandfather said so because when he was a little boy William Marsters the First used to buy things from traders who came to Palmerston, where they –' Cathy stopped to cough in the smoke from the campfire. 'And he paid with little heavy bags of gold coin that he took out of bottles that he kept buried in the ground.'

'How did he get those?'

'Nobody knows. But they were somewhere on Palmerston.'

'Where? Can we go and look?'

'No, Matthew. All the land's owned. They won't let you dig it up. Anyway it's *their* great-grandfather's — it's their treasure.'

A wail of disappointment. 'Bet it's not true.'

'We'll never know if it is or not,' said Cathy. 'Nobody's found it yet, and there are still about fifty living on Palmerston.'

In the next few days mysterious excavations appeared in lonely parts of Maina, but the bone-dry sand was difficult to move with Stacey's tiny plastic bucket and spade, and the craze for treasure hunting soon faded.

Stacey was not motivated by greed or romance. She stayed near the waterline, happily filling half a coconut with damp sand and tipping it out again.

When Kauraka had led Cathy and me round Rarotonga in 1989, he'd taken us to meet some friends. They were a big family of islanders who had a rambling plot of land away from the coast; one of them had married a Filipino woman who spoke good English. I remembered her saying how the Cook Islanders didn't know how lucky they were, because her own country had been raped by Western culture, but here in the Cooks they had a charmed life.

We were standing to one side of her yard when she told me this. There were chickens idling about in the sun, stabbing the ground occasionally for corn, and a dog was chained up nearby. I was trying to ignore what was going on. One of the men was killing a pig. It squealed, the sort of squeal you would make if you were dumb and a big creature seized you with knife upraised. Its tiny feet scratched hopelessly in the dust. Cathy went white and turned away towards me.

'You don't like it,' Kauraka said. 'Look. There are chickens on a lot of the islands; you may need to eat them. Watch me.' He stepped forward, agile despite his weight, and grabbed a chicken. He tucked it under his arm. It clucked and looked surprised. He took its neck in one chubby hand.

'Look.'

His hand was firm as a vice. The neck twisted, hung down limp. The legs kicked a few times.

I wouldn't dream of killing things at home. At home if you buy a chicken in the supermarket you'd never know it had ever breathed or had senses: it's just a cold clammy lump that goes flaky when you cook it. Yet here I felt I had a right to take what I wanted and feed my family on it. I could kill fish or chickens and not feel guilty about it. And there were chickens on Maina, at least forty of them, so all I had to do was catch one.

I put it off at first. Then I felt somehow that I couldn't really show that I cared for my family unless I did it. I wasn't very confident about catching it and picking it up as Kauraka had done. The chickens here were wild, they were not used to people and they shied away if you got really close.

So I invented a trap made out of the fishing net. Craig and Matthew and I hacked our way through the bushes to a clearing. There we weighted one end of the oblong net with stones and stretched the other ends up over sticks so that the chicken would walk into it, like a goal mouth. We laid a trail of coconut fragments into it. Then we waited. We sat nearby and played games with stones.

After a couple of hours a big brown hen came along, bobbing its head down all the time to pick at the bits of coconut. When it was well under we let the net fall. Craig and Matthew knelt on the sides and held them down taut over its feathers. I wanted to get this over with quickly. The thing didn't move under the net. I grabbed the neck and twisted hard. I gave silent thanks because I had done it right first time. Cathy plucked it and boiled it in coconut water, but it tasted rubbery and slimy with a whiff of crab.

Nevertheless, I – or, rather, the boys and I – had shown ourselves to be the true hunters within our little tribe on Maina.

Mosquitoes continued to be a problem. The children tried to sleep in the palm hut one night, but within half an hour they were traipsing back to camp, complaining about the pesky little creatures. I told myself that I would try to construct something stronger.

'I wish Gareth was here,' I said. 'We could do with a handyman.'

I had laid a mat of palm fronds well away from camp, to kneel and meditate on, and now Cathy and I were lying on it under a sun that bore down on us like a radiator. While the children rested in the afternoon we had some privacy here on the ocean side of the island.

'He'd need a bloody long extension for his Black & Decker,' Cathy said. 'Anyway what would he do for wood?

I can't see Palmer being too happy about Gareth felling trees all over the island.'

'You wouldn't need to fell trees,' I said. 'You could build a hut out of driftwood. Like William Marsters the First did for his wives. We could have a school hut and a sleeping hut and a love hut.'

'A *what* hut?'

'A love hut.'

'You're going on again,' she said.

'It's the coconut water: it makes you virile.'

'It's the tent you mean, it makes you frustrated.'

'Help me make a hut, then.'

And so we made a shelter under the palm trees. I thought about Kauraka and what he had told me about island marriages before the missionaries came, how a young man and a girl held hands in the bushes, and they were married.

It didn't take much longer than that for us to build a private place out of leaves, climb into it, and twine together in erotic passion, our skin smelling of the salt sea and coconut oil, our nakedness zebra-striped by the sun shining through the palm fronds.

'*Eeech!* ' yelled Cathy. I'm on a bloody trochus shell.'

As time progressed, the five of us evolved a pattern, like an elaborate dance: we spent time together, then drew apart and went our separate ways. In the mornings the children wrote or read or did sums from their schoolbooks in the hut; and as the sun went down they sat around the camp-fire and talked to us. Sometimes in the afternoon my hours of meditation would be interrupted by voices raised in the interior.

'No, you can't – it's Conan the Barbarian.'

'It's not if you let it go over the bridge – it'd be Superman; then it could have rescued Conan, look –'

'Get off! This is the bridge. Look, here, look, he can't fly. Craig, gimme it, gimme it, here, Craig.'

Then there was a slap and howl and I got up off the mat.

'What's going on in there? What you doing, you two?'

And Craig emerged red in the face.

'Matthew won't let me play with his figure men.'

'He makes them all stupid: he wants them to fly and they can't. Stupid. They can't fly. They're my figure men and it's my game.' Matthew puffed out his small bare chest and grabbed at the toy in Craig's hand. I had to hold my sons apart.

'I never quarrelled like this with my brother,' I said.

'Yeah, he never took things,' said Matthew, glaring.

'Yeah, he wasn't a big baby,' said Craig.

Cathy came crashing through the bushes. She wore a sarong all the time these days, and flip-flops, and I suddenly realised how different she looked, how much browner and stronger. It's strange how things happen before your very eyes – but progressively, gradually, so you don't always notice. Then it hits you suddenly.

'What's going on here?' Cathy demanded. 'I could hear you two right over the beach there. Craig, give that back to Matthew. Go on, give it. Matthew, you know what I told you. You've got to share your toys. Do you understand that, Matthew?'

'Yes,' said Matthew reluctantly.

'You can keep them. I don't want to play now anyway,' said Craig.

'Good.'

Matthew stuck out his tongue at Craig's retreating back. They set off in different directions and we stood and watched them.

'Where's Stacey?'

'She's by the tent. She's built a stage out of stones, the way Craig showed her. You've got to come and see it, she says. That's what I was coming over for.'

We skirted my meditation mat and started walking along the edge of the interior to the camp. A minute or two later we could see Stacey in the distance, squatting happily on the beach near the tent, absorbed in her game.

'It's a good thing we've got a lot of space,' Cathy said. 'Wish we had a back garden this size at home.'

'It's really good for self-expression, isn't it?'

'I was thinking more of getting away from each other.'

'No, it's all the space you need, Cath. Look, you can do what you want and there's nobody to say you shouldn't.' I was feeling very enthusiastic and as I talked to Cathy I leaped over a log without looking. A red-hot needle shot into my toe. My scream brought the children running.

'*Yeugh*.'

'Oooh, look at that.'

'What is it?' I had sat on the ground with my leg out straight and Cathy was looking at my toe.

'You're better off not knowing. Craig. Give me your T-shirt. No, keep your leg still, Tony – I'm going to get it out.'

Craig wriggled out of his T-shirt and Cathy used it to cover her hand. I felt a slight tug and squealed with pain.

'Stupid thing,' Cathy said, peering at my toe. 'Half of it's still in there.'

'Half of what?'

'You landed on this.'

In the folds of the T-shirt was half a shiny dark insect, something like a cross between a scorpion and a giant centipede.

'There's a long black bit under the skin.'

I hobbled back to camp supported on Cath's arm, and sat in the dust while the boys found fuel.

'Craig's getting good at climbing up for fire lighters, isn't he?' Cathy said conversationally, with her arm around my shoulder. Fire lighters were the dusty ribbons of copra that hung below the crown of the coconut palm.

I was too far gone in pain to bother with this sort of talk. My toe was slowly inflating, the skin stretching taut around the nail. I lifted the foot gingerly towards my nose and looked again at the long black string beneath the surface.

'Do you think you can get it out, Cath?'

'Stop asking daft questions.'

When the fire was started she boiled a needle from her sewing kit in the coconut water. I sat still, feeling my toe throbbing, and coughed slightly as gusts of smoke blew in my direction.

'You sit beside me with the limes, Stacey; there's a good girl. This might hurt, Tony.'

My wife approached the sole of my foot with a large needle. She poked it slowly into my toe and I winced. Craig and Matthew knelt beside me, watching.

'They used to have whisky,' Craig said.

'Who did?'

'In the Wild West. Cowboys, when they had to have a foot off.'

'Tony, keep still! Craig, I'll murder you if you say one more thing.'

Matthew was giggling.

'There! All out. Give us some lime juice, Stace.'

Cathy dabbed lime juice onto my toe as Tere had told us to if we got bitten. After that I sat and nursed my toe while Cathy got some fish from the lagoon and boiled it. Matthew sat beside me and asked questions about amputees, which gave Craig an excuse to do his Long John Silver impression. He caught my eye after a while and stopped.

Sometimes in the afternoons I used to hear Craig entertaining the other two. He was perfecting an American accent that he had learned playing Baby Face, a character in *Bugsy Malone*.

'Here comes the King of the Island,' Craig said. He was lying on his stomach with his chin in his hands, gazing at the big cockerel. It was like a rooster in a picture book – red and orange and yellow with a warty red crest and an imperious demeanour. It took one step towards us, hesitated and stepped back.

'That's Meg there. Look. Give us the cabin bread, Matthew,' said Cathy.

She wet a piece of bread in warm coconut water and gently put it in front of Meg, who was a plain brown chicken and 'wife' of the King. She stretched out a fat feathered leg gingerly, then another, then extended her neck down to peck at the bread.

'The lady hens are all dowdy,' said Cathy.

'Except for the little white one,' said Craig. 'She's a pretty chicken. Look, she's all fluffy.'

'The Prince is after her, see?' Cathy told him.

'He won't get her: the King won't let him.'

There was a hierarchy – you could see it. None of the chickens came scrabbling around after breakfast unless the King of the Island had been over first to take a look at us. And he never took any food: he considered it beneath him. He let his big sons and his 'womenfolk' grub about for bits of coconut and then he rounded them up and led them off into the bushes again.

Stacey had given Meg her name. She had six chicks, but fed and sheltered only five of them. The other one was a weakling: it had something wrong with its eyes. Craig had caught it, held it tenderly and bathed its eyes with Dettol and water, and it wobbled off uncertainly after the others.

A little red chicken led her four young ones, scrappy things still shedding fluff, into the clearing. She looked self-conscious, like a young matron who had dressed up to go to the shops because she knew the whole neighbourhood would be talking. She was about to take a piece of coconut when the Prince took a big step towards her and pecked sharply at her neck. He chased her squawking into the bushes.

'He's always doing that to her,' Cathy observed.

'She's his wife, he's jealous,' I reasoned.

'She's the one who wants to be jealous: he's after the pretty white chicken. Look, he's shameless. Bloody polygamist, he is.' Cathy directed this at me, laughing.

Craig said, 'See that black one there, with the red crest? He reminds me of somebody.'

'It's the way he walks, see,' I said. 'He stays on the sidelines and he won't look at you. He doesn't want to be with the others.'

'Looks like he's looking for dog ends in the gutter,' Cathy put in.

'He's got a surly look, hasn't he?' said Craig. 'It's Gordon – that's who he's like. He's a punk. Imagine him with a couple of chains linking his legs up.' Gordon was a boy who lived near to Cathy's parents. He was six foot tall with a ring through his nose and his hair in a rigid scarlet crest down the middle of his head, and he'd got black trousers on, with chains looped between thighs.

'When can we have some more chicken to eat?' Stacey asked. She had been the only one of us who liked the boiled chicken. 'I want chicken and chips and sauce.'

'You'll be lucky,' said Cathy.

'I don't want to kill another one, Stace,' I said. 'We've got to know them now – it's different.'

'Well, then just a leg,' Stacey persisted. Meg was peaceably pecking at the dust, but, as Stacey marched over, she looked up and squawked and stepped away.

'Look, we could have one leg. She'd still be able to hop.'

'*Yeugh!*'

The chicken cluck-clucked and made her way indignantly into the undergrowth.

The hens were like characters in a soap opera. We had

spent weeks watching how they looked after their babies, tucking them under their wings to sleep at night, and picking up bits of coconut that they disgorged tenderly into the mouths of the littlest ones.

Stacey felt no remorse about hunting dumb creatures and eating them. She particularly enjoyed pulling the fish out of the net by their heads. She sat on the sand, head down in concentration, ponytail bobbing, her tiny fingers deftly tugging the fish through the drift of white net.

Everybody else found this a fiddly job. At first she pulled them through the wrong way, by the tail, but that made the head and spine stay stuck in the net with most of the flesh.

I usually sat near her, taking the fish as she released them, gutting them with my fingers and throwing the waste into the lagoon for the crabs. Sometimes I ate a few raw fish as I worked. They had a pleasant chewy texture and tasted of the sea. With a bit of vinegar and pepper they would have been just like the cockles Cathy and I used to get in Swansea market when we were first going out together.

Ah, Swansea market! An infinity and an eternity away.

After all these weeks I should have felt settled. Cathy was happy and loving, Craig's sunburn had almost healed, Stacey liked the beach and Matthew seemed contented climbing for coconuts and playing ever more heavily plotted games with his figure men. I meditated every afternoon. Yet I was the one who still fidgeted and talked about the future as a time when everything would miraculously be better than it was now.

It was as if any stress at all, any feeling that some important watershed was approaching, spoiled my peace of mind. I wanted to feel that time had stood still. I couldn't settle down because I kept expecting other people to turn up on our island.

We were on a desert island, yet we were not abandoned. It was that feeling of being on our own, of controlling our own destiny, that I was looking for.

I was sitting on the sand near the water's edge, cleaning the net of its last few fish. It was that quiet time in the late afternoon when all the living things except us seemed to be enjoying the siesta. There was no sound at all, only the lapping waters of the lagoon and the soft hiss of the breeze in the palm tops. Everyone except me was in the shade by the tent, helping to build the fire, but from here I could not even hear them talking. The net was white against the white sand; I shut my eyes for a second and saw red netting against red sand.

The heat bored into my shoulders.

'Hullo?' said a man.

My heart turned over. I jumped to my feet. He was a tall white man in a baseball cap, a T-shirt that said 'ADIDAS' and shorts. He looked frightened when he saw my face. I suppose I looked a bit rough, with my growth of beard and sunburn scabs.

'Hello,' I replied. 'Who are you?'

'I come in my boat,' he said in a German accent. 'Why are you here? How do you come here?'

'We live here. There's my wife and children up there,' I said proudly.

He looked where I pointed. I suppose it looked less than idyllic, the tent with the washing and the water container outside and the suitcases, but I didn't expect him to look quite so shocked.

'Have a bit of fish?' I said cheerfully, and bit into a piece and offered him another. He pulled a face and made a disgusted take-that-away sort of motion with his hand.

'Well, go up and meet the family, why don't you?' I said.

Cathy had stood up now and so had all the children. They stood and stared at this stranger. He looked from them to me and back again.

'We've got a fire up there. You can have some fresh-cooked fish with us.'

He started walking hesitantly along the beach in the direction of the tent and I rinsed my hands in the lagoon and set off to follow him. As he drew level with the tent he didn't head for it, but started walking faster. Then, unexpectedly, he broke into a run. He grabbed his hat from his head and sprinted along the damp sand at the water's edge, his figure growing ever smaller until he disappeared round the far end of the island. Cathy jumped down the bank to meet me on the beach and the children crowded round.

'He looked petrified. What did you say to him, Tony?'

'Nothing.'

'You do look a bit wild. Your hair's all sticking up and you've still got those scabs.'

'He said he'd got a boat.'

'I'll go and look,' said Craig, and set off after the man, with Matthew in pursuit.

'They won't catch him now,' I ventured.

'Should hope not,' said Cathy. 'He looked white as a sheet. I think he thought he might be dinner.'

I followed the boys and was in time to see the man clambering aboard a small boat that he had anchored about thirty feet offshore. He disappeared into the cabin and a motor started. Smoothly the vessel wheeled away from us in the direction of One Foot Island. We watched for a while and then walked on, round the island, the way he had first approached us.

'Look,' said Matthew. 'He left prints in the sand, Dad.'

I stopped and looked where he was pointing.

'It's a good thing we saw him,' I said.

I wondered what I would have felt if I hadn't met the man face to face. Frightened maybe. I was feeling a bit vulnerable in any case. I had almost lulled myself into imagining we were living in seclusion, and we were not. We were 140 miles (225 kilometres) from Rarotonga, certainly, but our privacy was an illusion. We were still just across the lagoon from a tourist island.

That night I dreamed that I woke up because somebody was kicking my feet. I unzipped the tent and a microphone was shoved into my face. At the other end of it, grinning maniacally over a false beard, was a man in a trilby hat and a long raincoat.

'Hullo,' I said. Cathy's father was sitting behind the man on a sofa, roaring with laughter.

The cockerel began to crow. I opened my eyes wide and stared at the orange canvas glowing with sunshine. We had as usual changed position in the night, all chasing each other round in a kind of circle so that Stacey was now curled into a corner and the rest of us were sprawled in a swastika with our feet kicking uncomfortably together. There was a crab just outside the zip; that was what I had felt against my feet. I prodded gingerly and the canvas went flaccid again.

I struggled out of the tent, took a deep breath of cool air and slid down the bank to the beach. You had to be careful crossing it this early, because sometimes scores of hermit crabs were still about. The didn't go into their burrows until it got hotter. I always thought I might get one hanging onto my toe, like on a seaside postcard.

The lagoon water was tepid and refreshing, and I walked out until it was up to my chest. It would have been nice to just belly-flop into it and swim, but I had given up trying a long time ago. Cathy had tried to teach me at the Leisure Centre when we'd got back to Swansea last time and I never managed it. You feel a bit of a fool trying to kick your legs out with your wife holding your hands and old-age pensioners gasping past in shoals, doing the breast-stroke. Their skin always looked like crêpe, as if they'd been in there all afternoon. And I had a horror of putting my head under water. Cathy said I should be able to do that and I could start in the bath, but I prefer to have a shower at home. Matthew's the same, frightened of the water. Cathy tried to teach him as soon as we got to Maina but he wasn't interested.

Craig lived in the water, like a porpoise. He would go off and swim on his own and we had to make him promise not to do it without one of us knowing.

A few weeks after the German tourist had arrived so unexpectedly, it was Craig, in the lagoon, who spotted Tere's boat.

With her arrival, our time on Maina was coming to an end. We did become castaways again for a short period of time. But by the end of 1995 we eventually left the Cook Islands.

As I sat on the veranda of my two-room hut on Rarotonga, I dozed as I contemplated our stay on Maina, our island of dreams: the timeless days, the sunburn, the fish and the chickens, the arrival of the newspapermen, the frightened German tourist, the crabs, the heat – and, of course, the hurricane. Although frightening to us, the winds we had experienced couldn't be compared to the disastrous devastation caused by Cyclone Martin.

I was brought out of my reverie as a cool breeze surrounded my body. But I felt so comfortable that I decided to sleep there for the night.

8

Aunts and Uncles

This was a beautiful time of day as the shadows length-
ened and the sun became redder in the clear sky, spray-
ing the sea with a rich and resplendent crimson dappled
with dancing light. I was husking a coconut when Miari
appeared. It had been three days since her last visit.

'This is for you.' She smiled as she handed me a bunch
of bananas and two avocados. 'We can take them with us.'

'To where?' I enquired.

'To the *motu*. I need to get away for a while and it's a
good place to finish the story. Nobody lives there – we'll
have the island to ourselves. It's still light so we can leave
straightaway.'

The only things I took apart from the fruit were my
recorder and a hammock. We got on Miari's 100cc motor-
cycle, which would take us to Muri beach about seven miles
(11 kilometres) away, travelling on the inner circular road –
an ancient pathway called the Ara Metua. She drove and I
sat behind holding on to her slim waist for support, listening to the bike's snarling, whining, occasionally sputtering
progress. Her hair had blown into my face; it gave the

heady aromas of musk and coconut oil.

No boat was needed, since, at certain times of the day, the lagoon was low enough to walk through. We waded across the warm waters that reached shoulder height, our belongings held aloft in backpacks.

We had come to this *motu* because Miari felt some kind of safety here, away from her confused home life. Across the waters everything was peaceful. She loved that. She controlled her own life here. She loved *her* little island, as she called it.

Miari knew exactly where to put up the hammock, between two palm trees, just on the edge of the interior facing the open sea.

We settled ourselves and lit a small fire. Miari got comfortable in the hammock, and started her story. Her words were coming out like machine-gun bullets, as though I were the only person she'd ever been able to talk to and she had to say as much as she could in a short time. Perhaps she did think this. Or perhaps it was because I was a stranger, that guy from Britain. It's often easier to offload your close and personal thoughts to someone you don't know. That small quirk of being human is what, after all, keeps psychoanalysts fat and healthy.

Miari turned onto her side and the wraparound skirt, the *pareu*, that she wore around her slim body parted slightly, revealing her long dark legs. Gracefully, she got out of the hammock with an ease that suggested she'd slept in nothing else. She moved elegantly, and settled beside me on the sand, looking into my face with her large brown eyes. I could see why so many Europeans had fallen in love with these innocent-looking Polynesians. Their faces radiated a kind of purity and simplicity, while their bodies spoke of pleasures promised.

One such European had been William Marsters, a ploughboy from Gloucestershire, who ran away to sea in 1858. Setting sail from Bristol, on a three-masted sailing ship, bound for Australia, he couldn't have been happy because he jumped ship at Penrhyn (also called Tongareva), which is one of the northern group of the Cook Islands. It seems that the islanders of Penrhyn were not at all happy to have this newcomer in their midst.

However, one young warrior helped him build a canoe, and waved him away as he paddled out to sea. Marsters must have been given good directions, because he fetched up on Palmerston, another of the Cook Islands, in the southwest. By the early 1860s he was settled there with his wife, who was a local girl. He later took two more wives, and, by the time he died at the end of the nineteenth century, his three wives had borne him scores of children and there were hundreds of grandchildren, all of them bearing his name. It was his descendants who had helped me and my family to become castaways.

I wanted to hear Miari's story more or less from the beginning, or as far back as she could remember. I began:

'When did you first leave Rarotonga?'

'Well I have several brothers and sisters, all older. My eldest brother who was fifteen at the time became really ill, and so my mum had to find somebody to look after me. I was about two then. So it was this family that was baby-sitting me at the time, and they grew attached to me during those times when my mum was at the hospital. But three months later my brother died, and the family that looked after me were moving to New Zealand, and so they asked if they could adopt me. I don't know the full story, but I was sent to New Zealand with the family.

'There were four of us kids in the same bed, in a double bed. I don't know how we slept, but somehow we did. It was a three-bedroomed house. There'd be four of us in one bedroom, two adults in the next room with two kids, and my auntie and uncle in the other room – my mum and dad I called them: you know, the ones that took care of me.

'Did you ever think: Where's my real mum and dad?'

'Well I was thinking about that, but no, not really, because they weren't exactly, like, excluded from the family. Every chance they actually had to come over to New Zealand they came. And I was young then.

'I remember my fifth birthday. My dad came over then and he bought me a paint set. It just didn't seem important because I always thought that the family I was with were my family, and my mum and dad were always my mum and dad, but they were always over in Raro. So, no. And, apart from the fact there were so many of us, we were used to sharing. I mean, we had no choice [but to accept] such a lifestyle. Yeah, but the thing that really got me, I mean now looking back, is that, if they couldn't afford to look after so many kids, why bother. I mean, we suffered during that whole period. I really hated it. The conditions weren't as bad, but, you know, we could have had a better life.

'I remember the parties in New Zealand. My aunties and uncles thought they'd have, like, massive parties because, you know, Cook Islanders are just free and lovely: they just love to have parties, and drink too much. And I remember my uncle. We would all be in the sitting room, and sleeping on the floors and stuff. He'd come around and play with one of the girls. We were only about ten years old at the time. He would talk to her and touch her, and we would all be lying there kinda like still, so he doesn't come to us. And she would say, "Don't, Uncle," and he'd go, "Oh, it's OK, don't worry about it. I'm just playing. Let Uncle play."

'Things like that happened a lot. The parents didn't bother: they were too much into their social life. It was only during parties things like that happened. The uncles that would come over to the function, yeah, they were the abusers. It wasn't the ones within the household. It was the other ones. I remember at one of the parties, one of the aunties, she sat – she sat on the sink and peed, man. Oh it was so disgusting.'

'She did it in front of everyone?' I asked, incredulous.

'Oh, yeah, everybody could see her. She was so pissed, man. I remember standing there and trying to carry her out, 'cos she fell into the sink, and she was still peeing all over the place. That was the worse.

'We had to learn to look after ourselves very quickly back then. And all we did then, too, was look after the younger kids, and clean up the house. So I learned how to, like, clean a house up, wash the clothes, dishes and so forth. I looked after a kid when I was seven – you're trained very young. You become very independent quickly. You know, even though I was in New Zealand, if you were a Cook Islander you live as you would if you were in the islands, because people from the Cook Islands were just flying over to New Zealand around the mid-1970s, when the airstrip was built. That's when everyone started flying over, and their ways went with them.

'It's not until now that our generation are turning it around, apart from the law, and putting a stop to it. Yeah, the women can speak up more. You can't get away with abusing your kids – although I did learn through those abusers. I find that kids now are getting so spoiled and lazy, whereas back then, before we went to school in the mornings, we'd wake up, clean up the house. We had to get the house all clean. The kitchen, the sitting room, our beds and bedroom had to be totally immaculate before we left; otherwise we'd get a really good hiding.

'And we had to clean it before we went to school. Doesn't matter how late you get. And then, when you get to school, 'cos you're late you get detention, and then you're angry and often you start swearing and your teacher's, like, putting a peg on the tip of your tongue because you swore. I can't believe I swore. I just remembered that too.

'And we used to go to school with cabin bread – you know, cabin-bread sandwiches. OK just cabin bread, butter and jam slabbed together, and that was lunch. So my cousin, she used to look out for me and she used to steal other kids' school lunch, and we'd go around the corner and just like eat up. That's how we basically lived. She would steal other kids' stationery and pencils because we couldn't afford to buy them.'

'So why did this family take on other people's children if they couldn't afford them?' I asked Miari.

'Habits – from grandparents' habits that are slowly dying out now,' she said. 'Yeah, mothers are becoming more responsible for their own children, only because of the way they've been treated, through adopters; well they call them feeding families. Yeah, through feeding families, anyway, they have their favourites and then you have the slave of the family. There's always, like, one child who's the slave. I remember one guy, I won't mention his name, but he would do all the dirty work. He'd be the one to wake and do the breakfast for everyone, and clean up the dishes while the others went to school. And he'd have to weed the garden and clean up the garden. He'd get beaten up so badly. Yeah, he was treated like an animal.'

'How old was he?'

'He was our age at the time. He was six. And that family wanted to adopt me. They would beat him because he didn't do something right.'

'They kept him home from school, so that he could do all the work?'

'Yeah, because he had too many chores to do, so he couldn't go to school. Apart from the fact he'd get beaten anyway, so the bruises would show. So, yeah, it wasn't exactly glamour.'

'So what became of him?'

'Oh now he's – he actually left that place and went back to his birth parents' place, back here, to the Cook Islands.

Now he's doing so well. He's got his own family, and he's just enjoying being with his real family.'

'Did most feeding families do things like that?'

'Just some of them, because – I don't know what it was, but because they were so used to bringing up so many kids, that there was always one they would pick on. It would be the slow one, too – yeah, mentally slow.'

'But the slow ones need more encouragement and love!'

'Yeah, exactly.'

'But he wasn't slow, though, was he?'

'Well he was actually mentally slow; I think it was because of all the head bashing. Yeah, everybody used to tease him.'

'And when they used to hit him they used to really slap him?'

'Oh, no, nothing like that, no. They used to get, like, a four-by-four wood sometimes and whack him across the head, quite a few times. And around the back – no, really beat him up, until he couldn't walk – and then that would be enough. This is the sort of hidings we would get – we called them hidings.'

'But you never had any of that, did you?'

'Hell, yes!'

'What was the worst you had?'

'The worst? OK, you know that thing you use to sharpen knives, that metal part and it's got a handle. Well that, yeah, we used to get whacked on the arms with it. Hell, yeah, that hurt: it's metal, it was heavy. But apart from that we'd get whacked behind the legs with a brush from a dustpan and brush, the wooden one. Oh, man, such sensitive areas, 'cos they really know where to hit you after a while.

'And they use to hit you with a wooden spoon, yeah, but that kept breaking, so they went for harder stuff. 'Cos, see, as you gradually grow, things start to break, so they had to, like, get something else that was more solid, and after a while you just get so numb that it doesn't hurt you any more.

'Then I started to rebel. I would lie about where I was going. I got a really good beating if I didn't do something right at that time. I was seeing guys; I would say I was doing homework at friends', and because I came back at about 2 a.m. she would beat me on the legs with wooden clogs. I got so angry and upset that I decided to run away. I made my way to my sister's house, in another part of New Zealand, and I lived with her for a while. She was my real sister.

'I couldn't concentrate in school at all; I wanted to be doing other things. So I was eventually sent over to Rarotonga.'

'What age were you?'

'I was fifteen then. I remember one time, not long after I'd got there, I'd just got home; it was late and I jumped into bed ... In Raro the houses are, like, left open, you know, the doors and stuff ... And my bedroom door was slightly closed, and this guy comes knocking on my door and I thought it was my brother-in-law, but it was his neighbour. He comes waltzing in the door and starts touching my feet, it was quite dark, and I still thought it was my brother-in-law and so I kicked him. I turned around and realised it wasn't him.

'I was, like, half naked: I only had my underwear on, 'cos the houses are just like boxes – there's nothing to them man. Because it's so humid and hot, there's no need to have windows. So I said "Don't," and I turned around and he was there and I'm, like, "Who are you?" and he says, "Is so-and-so here?" I thought: Fuck, no, there's this stranger on the end of my bed that's about to rape me. Oh my God. I was half naked. I just pulled up the sheet and covered myself. Thankfully, he just left. That was bloody scary.'

9

What Cinderella Did
After the Ball

It was quite early when I decided to explore the *motu*, which wasn't much more than about half a mile long. I'd been tossing and turning for hours, whether it was due to the sand flies or my overactive mind I don't know, but eventually I decided to take a walk. I left Miari fast asleep in the hammock. I didn't want to wake her as we had talked into the early hours. I decided I would surprise her with some coconuts for breakfast.

The interior reminded me of a miniature rainforest – bushes and shrubs mingled together – and, without the aid of a large stick I'd found, it would have been almost impossible to penetrate the dense growth. I found another use for the stick further inland: the coconut trees were a little higher than I thought so I used it for knocking down the nuts.

By the time I'd returned Miari was already up, and it looked as if she'd had the same idea as I'd had concerning breakfast. She had already cut up the avocados. I handed her the coconuts and she gave me the bananas. While I peeled those she husked the coconuts. The sun was giving off a blistering heat as we gulped down the refreshing water from the nuts.

This was going to be our one day together alone in paradise, sharing our thoughts. Our first thought was to cool off in the lagoon. As Miari swam with ease in the crystal-clear waters, I just stood there, water up to my chest. Miari found this quite funny: for the islanders swimming is a way of life. I splashed her when she laughed a second time. This made her laugh even more and I wasn't surprised when she retaliated. I was glad that she felt relaxed around me. We had found a friend in each other.

As we dried ourselves out on the beach, Miari continued her story.

'Did you know I was married once? Just for a short time.'

'No. How did you meet him?'

'He was a tourist. I met him at a dance on Raro and we danced all night. I made sure I danced with him – not that he could dance, but, you know, he can't help his breed!' This was her way of saying white men are bad dancers. 'I'm sure I showed him a step or two, and then I kissed him passionately outside. I was so sick because I had to run: I had my friend's bike at the time and she finished work at 12 p.m. And so I had to go. It was like Cinderella really: I had to run after such a good time.

'And he started to run around to see where I worked, and then he found me. He was having a party that weekend and my friend and I went to his place, and I told him exactly what I wanted to do – no, what I liked in a relationship and what I didn't like and whether he liked it or not, and he agreed with it. So we went ahead and I bonked him that night, and I ended up marrying him.

'Oh, that's a long story, though. I mean, I didn't exactly want to marry him immediately. But he brought it up. He thought it would be a lot easier, a lot cheaper, for him, too, because he had to pay thirty dollars a month to extend his stay and he was tired: he was tired of, like, having to do that 'cos it'd been eight months now, and he says, "Well, we're going to be together anyway." And I'm, like, "Yeah, but marriage, that's commitment." Not that I minded at the time but then, when you start bringing money into it, I thought: My God, this guy's trying to marry me so that he can stay here. But that wasn't the case, and so I married him.

'My husband and I then went to the States. His dad wanted to build a business because he sold his house and everything, and they came to Rarotonga to find business. He couldn't find one in the Cook Islands because everything seemed so unsure and everybody was asking for unreasonable prices, so he decided to go elsewhere. So we went to Hawaii. They used to live there when my husband was young. I didn't want to go because I felt uncomfortable going and not being able to support myself, 'cos I had no money at the time. God, I was dead broke.

'His dad insisted on his son going, but his son wouldn't go without me and so I had to go. So I went. No regrets. I had a wonderful time. I had a great time actually. I just didn't know it at the time.

'Hawaii. Oh, man, there are so many waterfalls. I just love waterfalls. They're just so beautiful. There are just so many of them. You hike or drive up the mountains, up the canyon. Oh, man, it was just breathtaking, 'cos I love countryside. That's why I love the Cook Islands. My husband and I, every chance we'd get, we'd try and go through different trails, see how far it would take us, you know.

'Sometimes we'd go on a Kawasaki one hundred cc. We would drive up those hills, you know. I'd get so scared sometimes. I'd jump off and he'd say, "No, hang on." It actually made it up those hills – I couldn't believe it.

'Yeah, so we pretty much had something in common. We loved the countryside. And he was a good husband: he was always there to provide for us.

'He took me over to San Francisco. The first time I was there, man, it blew me away. I just wanted to live there – I loved it. So we made sure we went over to San Francisco every weekend. We tried to catch trips over to Alcatraz but couldn't because they were always constantly booked out.

'Anyway, we went sightseeing elsewhere, like the Golden Gate Bridge. My husband especially liked to visit this certain place: it's like a hippie street, it's a long street. You see people in their sixties and seventies gear, with bell-bottoms and stuff, selling drugs. And, because my husband and his dad enjoyed it so much, we'd go there all the time, and because I liked San Francisco I wouldn't mind.'

'Does his father take drugs too?'

'His dad used to be an alcoholic about twenty years prior to that. He stopped drinking completely but then turned to drugs. He says it isn't the same thing: it's a natural herb, it's fine, it's cool! And I'm thinking: Man, you're a dope. And my husband was turning out to be exactly like him.

'From there we went to Sacramento to meet his mother, at Lake Tahoe. Such a beautiful place. Oh, man, if I become rich I'm gonna build a place there. It's the most beautiful place. It was just like how on TV you see these pine trees and streams and snow and cottages and stuff. Oh, man, now *that's* America. Everything else just seems the same, because I've been to Japan and stuff – you know, concrete city. Everything was great for a while, but his dad was paying for almost everything because he wanted his son to have just about most things. My husband did some odd jobs just to get some extra cash, but apart from that we were dependent on his father.

'I was getting stressed out because I wanted to go back to work, but I didn't want to work in the States. I'd heard so many stories over the TV, one about a lady being found dead outside this bar after she'd closed up or something like that. I know I shouldn't listen to that kind of bullshit, but you do.

'And so we decided to come back to Rarotonga. Our relationship had started to go downhill by now. It wasn't working out at all, only because his dad started organising our lives. Do you know, I was so happy and relieved to get back to Raro, because his dad had the cash? So, really, he was the one who was in control.

'So I was relieved to be back on Rarotonga because I could actually take control of my own life – or our own lives – and do what we wanted: find a place of our own, all lovey-dovey. But his dad, him and his dad found this place, a house in front of his dad's. Before I'd even seen it his dad had put a bond down, and got it all ready for us to live in. He organised everything. I was so pissed off because it was mine and my husband's chance to, like, do it on our own, but still we had this overhead of paying his dad back with this bond. I mean, he lived next door. The last thing I needed was for him to run our lives.

'I started working a lot. I would do night shift and he would do day. He would go out constantly and we rarely got to see each other. And then I got to a point where I spoke my mind. I said something that I shouldn't have. I got really angry and told him that he should have married his father instead of me; he should, like, go and wank his dad, or something like that – really, really disgusting. And he actually told his dad. You *believe* that? He told his dad. I was so mad at the time – there was no need for him to tell his father – and so we separated.

'Then his dad was going back to the States and he asked his son to go with him, and my husband went.

'While we were separated I had an affair. He was a local and it lasted for about two weeks. Oh, he had such a body: I mean, you know, those body-builders have those perfect breasts and ribs. Oh, his was like a washboard, man. I couldn't believe my luck [that] it was, like, me [he'd chosen]! Yes, it was me. So we went out, we went to so many parties. And everybody kept saying, "You're bonking him – you're bonking him?" And I wasn't, until I got fed up with people saying it, so I thought I'd make the rumours true and I did. Well, it was great sex anyway; yeah, I had such a great time.

'I remember one time we were cruising home from this beach party down on Muri beach. I was on the back of his bike and I was totally pissed. He didn't drink at all, you know, because he was watching his body. That's good: more for me! Yeah, I was on the back of his bike and I wore these flared trousers and this, like, little shortie top, and, mmm, I started caressing him while he was driving, distracting him. And then I just completely took my top off. By this time we were in town. I did it because he dared me to, and so I just took my top off. I mean, you couldn't exactly see my breasts 'cos he was covering them. That was too funny; it was pretty much a big thrill.

'Well, when you're drunk and you're happy and everything's going fine these things can happen. Yeah, those were the days.

'And so I went out with this guy for a couple of weeks, and then I had a phone call from my husband and a week later I left for New Zealand to go and see him. Me and that other guy stayed friends, though. He was really nice to me.

'I told my husband that I'd screwed; I'd actually screwed somebody else. He had heard something from his dad but I denied everything when he'd asked me over the phone, and when I got to New Zealand he asked me again, and I thought I'd tell him the truth. My husband got so pissed off; I'd never seen him so mad. He eventually calmed down and we stayed in New Zealand for about six months, but it just didn't work out, 'cos he didn't know how to express himself. Like, I would constantly ask him, "What's on your mind? You know, let it out." But he didn't know how to say it. Instead he would smoke pot.

'During his breaks he would come home, because we only lived down the road from where he was working. He'd come home for lunch and smoke pot. When he'd get up in the mornings the first thing he did was to go into the lounge and smoke a joint and when he'd come home in the evenings he'd go to his mate's place and just dope out. I'd be totally mad at him because he'd work during the day and I'd work in the evenings, so we hardly got to see each other. Our relationship pretty much ended then.'

Miari and I were getting ready for our return to the main island. I looked around, checking that we hadn't left anything behind. All that remained was the ashes of the burned-out campfire.

I gazed at that fire now, and thought of colder climes, of star-spangled nights on a prairie, wrapped and huddled against the subzero temperatures, needing the fire for warmth as well as for cooking on.

This seems as good a point as any to move on to our family's travels to a very different part of the world, where we went in search of a legend.

Interlude

I did say I was a traveller. The wanderlust was in my very essence. And this is one of those points in my multifaceted story where we digress and I take you on a very different journey – a journey from my native Wales to the United States of America.

Anyway, stories *should* feel spontaneous, and are apt to be discursive things, digressing here and there. For me, it's what makes them interesting.

But before we launch into our adventures in tracing the man who 'found' America before Columbus did – or so I firmly believe – I need to provide a bit of background.

During the evening on our desert island the children's thirst for knowledge had grown. They needed stories for their following day's performance – Matthew's figure men play-acting the scenes. The stories were told – as tradition demands – around the campfire. The story most in demand was the legend of Madoc, a Welsh prince who in the twelfth century left Wales with three hundred followers and settled in America, three hundred years before Columbus. Both my and Cathy's stories on Madoc were quite in-depth: we had researched the subject thoroughly. We had even visited the burial place of Prince Madoc's father, Owain Gwynedd, at Bangor.

While Owain was fighting battles for his people and their land, Madoc was displaying a love for the sea, his views on many things differing greatly from those of his father. It's thought that it was his ever-growing disillusionment with matters at home and the quarrelling among his brothers that eventually drove him from Wales.

When Owain's father died in 1137, Owain ascended the throne of North Wales. During the reign of King Stephen, which ended in 1154, Owain ruled successfully, extending his boundaries almost to the city of Chester. It was Henry II, who succeeded Stephen, who challenged Owain in 1157 – but failed in the ensuing battle. Eventually an agreement was reached: Owain would withdraw to Rhuddlan and the river Clwyd, and render homage.

These terms were kept until 1165. Henry and his forces were defeated by a combination of strong Welsh forces and bad weather at the Battle of Berwyn. As a result of such victories, the Welsh regained control of the border country.

The independence he secured in North Wales was maintained during Owain's lifetime, but succeeding generations, of course, would not be up to the task of retaining independence for Wales. In particular, one son – Dafydd, Madoc's brother – brought about a regime that disillusioned and terrorised many. He outlawed and exiled some of his brothers and may well have threatened Madoc's life.

Prince Madoc decided Wales was not the place for him. So it was that he left the land where his father Owain had been a great legend, and became a leader of his people not in Wales but across the Atlantic. Ironically, Madoc's descendants, and those of the people he took with him to America, had several hundred years of independence, while Wales lost hers in 1282 with the death of Llewelyn, Wales's last leader. As for Madoc and his followers they eventually, over a period of time, merged with the natives, probably the Sioux, and became the Mandans.

The last time we were together as a travelling family had been the end of 1995. We had left the Cook Islands and set off on Madoc's trail and found ourselves on an Indian reservation in North Dakota. We learned that we were the first people to actually ask the Mandans what they thought of the connection between them and the Welsh.

We uncovered evidence never seen before, so fascinating that a film producer from London decided to make a documentary for BBC2's *Timewatch* series, based on our research and evidence.

10

The Story of the Three Tribes

The town of Minot (pronounced *my*-nott) into which we flew is home to more than 34,000 people. The houses we saw there were all detached, most of cabin-style design, and the first thing we noticed about the people was that they were very friendly, many of them greeting us spontaneously with a sociable 'Hi'. Compared with that of most American cities and towns, traffic here is slight. This was just as well: it was the first time I'd driven on the 'wrong' side of the road. We were bound for New Town, which is in the Fort Berthold reservation.

The reservation is not the original Fort Berthold. On 24 December 1862 the Sioux burned down Fort Berthold. Fort Atkinson was owned by the American Fur Company, who had owned the Fort Berthold fur-trading post, so Fort Atkinson was now occupied and renamed Fort Berthold.

At New Town we were looking for the Tribal Administration Office, and had come to see one Ed Lone Fight. I had contacted him by letter before our visit and he had invited us to come to the reservation, saying he would be glad to meet us any time. We saw the signpost for the reservation office. It was a one-storey building.

Immediately we were met by the friendly but curious looks of the Native Americans who were around the main entrance. A man who seemed to be in charge of the reception area approached us.

'Can I help you?'

'Yes,' I said. 'We're looking for Ed Lone Fight.' I produced a copy of the letter I'd received from him. 'Is he here?'

'His office is down there,' said the official. 'Follow me.'

And we did. The five of us trailed after him, feeling a little self-conscious under the stares of the Native Americans around us. We went down a small corridor until we came to two native women standing at a doorway. Our guide pointed to the older of them and said, 'That lady will help you.'

I smiled and thanked him; he nodded and walked away. I approached the woman he'd pointed out to us and showed her the letter.

'Ed's not here today,' she said. I think she could see the disappointment on my face. 'He's in a meeting in Washington. He won't be able to meet with you until tomorrow, but I'm his assistant, Sue. Maybe I can help you.'

I told her we were here to do research on the connection between the Mandans and the Welsh. She listened with interest, then said, 'OK, I'll try to put you in touch with some people who may be able to help you.' But first, she asked, would we like to watch the Appreciation Day celebration? It would add some colour and interest to our researches, she assured us.

'Well, yes, why not?' I said, and then looked at Cathy. She shrugged, smiled and gave me a 'Why not?' sort of look. Sue seemed happy with our decision, and showed us into a small hall, with chairs set out in rows facing two long tables at the front.

We learned that this was a special occasion in honour of Dr Wilson, who had arrived from Canada forty-three years before and had been the doctor to the natives here ever since. We watched, fascinated.

At first there was a naming ceremony, in which Dr Wilson and his wife, Lillian, were given native names in honour of their service to the community. Dr Wilson was named One Who Heals, while Lillian was given the title Woman Who Assists Many. Then there were tributes from tribal leaders and Dr Wilson was praised for all his achievements over the years. Plaques were presented to him and his wife, along with pictures, a quilt and a spectacular and resplendent headdress. But the climax, for me, at any rate, was the tribal dancing that followed. Three Native Americans played drums with such energy and emotion, and yet with the sort of disciplined precision that has you feeling the warmth of nascent tears behind your eyes. They also sang in their native tongue, luring us, transporting us, into a completely different world.

I looked around at Cathy, and I could see that she was moved, too. Even the children kept their eyes firmly on the players and dancers, mesmerised, captivated by the driving rhythms that pummelled the air and the dervish-like whirling and spinning of the dancers. It was an experience I'll not forget in a hurry.

After the excitement was over, we were given an old medicine bottle containing sweets, as a memento of the day. Sue asked us to wait while she went off to see somebody else, and we sat in a sort of stunned silence, with those drumbeats still ringing in our ears, and observed the people around us.

They reminded me very much of the Cook Islanders, with their warm smiles and trusting ways. As I looked at my children and wife, I thought back to how, in the Cook Islands, we had dressed in shorts and T-shirts. I thought of how we'd all sat in the clear lagoon trying to cool off after our crab races, under the blistering sun. Now we were sitting in our thick coats, hats and gloves in temperatures of five degrees. A far cry from the Pacific, but as far as I was concerned it was just as fulfilling.

My reverie was interrupted by Cathy. She always seems to do that – nudge me into wakefulness when my mind has drifted off to another universe.

'Where d'you think Sue's got to?' she asked.

'I don't know,' I replied. 'Probably seeing some people about us.'

No sooner were the words out of my mouth than she appeared.

'Come with me,' she said enthusiastically, like a child wanting to show Mum and Dad a new toy. 'I have someone I'd like you to meet.'

We followed her to a table at the side of the hall, and there sat a distinguished grey-haired Native American. Sue introduced us.

'Tony, Cathy, this is Luther Grinnell,' she said. 'He's half Mandan, half Hidatsa.'

It seemed odd to be introduced to someone and be told his tribal lineage in the same breath. Not the sort of introduction we were used to in Swansea. (Hello, this is Geraint. He's half Llanelli and half Merthyr Tydfil.)

'Hello,' Cathy and I said in unison.

'Hi.' Luther beamed at us as he stood up to shake our hands. He was a tall man – over six foot – and obviously strong and powerful. His short hair was silver grey and it topped a friendly, welcoming, bespectacled pair of eyes canopied by dark, bushy brows. 'Come outside,' he said.

We followed Luther outside the hall, pulling our collars up against the cold. He led us towards the bank of the river, the Missouri. 'Your children are happy children,' he said as we walked. Although the day was cold, it was sunny and clear, crisp and invigorating. 'Let's sit here,' he said at last. I expected that the children would want to wander off and explore, but they seemed fascinated by our newfound friend. Stacey drank water from the round flask we had brought with us. She offered some to Luther.

'Ah, water, yes,' he said, displaying a sort of reverence for a commodity we very much take for granted. He drank, and handed the flask back to Stacey, who looked down shyly as he smiled his thanks to her.

'Sue tells me you are Celtics,' Luther said at last. He had seemed in no hurry to get down to the business of our trip. It was as though he were saying by this gesture that we need not be hurried, that there was all this time in the world, and we could afford to be relaxed and tell our story in our own good time.

We told him why we were here, that we had been sent a letter by Ed Lone Fight, whom we were due to meet the following day, that we were chasing a legend that some historians had tried to debunk. Luther nodded, as if he were expecting all this, knowing with our every word what we were going to say next. Then he began to tell us his own story.

'My grandfather had a warrior name,' Luther Grinnell began solemnly, with the practised voice of a storyteller: 'Black Fox. As an elder his name was Black Chest. He told me of the moving islands, the ships that came over here and landed in our country, and he said the people who would become the Mandans landed at the mouth of the Mississippi river.'

By now our family group was captivated, and Luther had spoken only a few sentences.

'My grandfather said they went up the Ohio River valley – clear to the end of it. The land wasn't any good for planting corn, so they came back, and when they settled in North Dakota other Indians noticed that some Mandans had blue eyes, and some had blond hair.'

Luther explained that hundreds of years later – in 1738 – an explorer and fur trader called Pierre Gaultier de la Verendrye came looking for these people, having become intrigued by stories he'd heard. He visited the village of what he called 'the Mantannes'.

'He came right up here, and at a river called Little Knife River he found the Hidatsa tribe, and thought they were the Mandans. But there was a misunderstanding due to the sign language, and they found that the Mandans were downriver. Verendrye went downriver and found the Mandans. He stayed with them and wrote about the differences between them and other Native American peoples.'

What was significant, Luther said, was that he found the language of this strange tribe to be very similar to that of the Welsh people. And there was a striking similarity in the way they built their homes.

'When the Mandans eventually settled down here in

Bismarck and Mandan,' said Luther, 'they had earth lodges. That looks like a Celtic-type thing of old, you know.'

Luther then went on to speak about the city of Mandan.

'It's right across the river from Bismarck, about a hundred and sixty-five miles [265 kilometres] from here. Bismarck is our capital city here in North Dakota, and Mandan is where the Mandans used to live. There are no Indians there now, but they do have some earth lodges. There's a place called Fort Lincoln. It's where Custer – General Custer – where his fort was. He didn't get killed there: he got killed in Montana – Little Big Horn.'

Luther paused a moment, and looked at the sky. We were so fascinated by now with his story that we had almost forgotten how cold it was.

'The Mandans lived in earth lodges,' he repeated, 'and I'm guessing about 1890, because the last village – which was called Like-a-fish-hook village, near Garrison – is under water now. That place had earth lodges, too. They were moved to Elbowoods – which is also now inundated – around 1890, and they lived in cabins after that. There were only about four earth lodges left on the reservation at that time. They built new ones as they moved up here. That was probably in the 1890s or 1900s, when they had those, 'cause I was born in 1922 and those old Indians were still living then, in 1922.

'We're Americans now, but a lot of people don't feel good about it. They were independent until they were conquered. They've never really settled to it spiritually, you know, so they still have some of their culture, still have some of their traditions, and they still have their language.

'I can speak Hidatsa fluently,' Luther continued. 'But I didn't learn to speak English till I was seven years old.'

I took advantage of a pause in Luther's monologue and asked, 'What's happened to the Mandan language now? Have they lost it?'

'There are a few left who can still speak Mandan,' Luther said.

'On this reservation?' I asked, hoping against hope that the answer would be yes. And it was.

'Yes, in Mandan country at Twin Buttes. See, this reservation is divided into five segments, because the lake, Sakakawea, comes right through the middle of it, and cuts it off into five districts. The southern district – about a hundred miles [160 kilometres] from here – that's Twin Buttes area.'

Luther said there were several Indians there who still knew the Mandan language. Suddenly an image sprang into my mind of a group of people determined to cut themselves off from modernity and live according to their proud traditions. I couldn't resist asking Luther, 'Are there any reservations in America that still live as they used to? Do any of them live as they did in the past? And have any kept their old traditions?'

'No, no,' said Luther, not surprised at my question. He'd probably been asked it a hundred times before. 'They're into modern technology. They farm with machinery, harvest with machinery. But some of them still carry on their gardens like they used to, way back. I do that. I put in a garden. I've got some Hidatsa beans and Mandan corn.'

'What about buffalo?' I asked. 'Are there still any buffalo?'

'Buffalo?' Luther smiled. 'Oh yeah, we have a buffalo herd. It belongs to the tribe. We have a big fence around it, along the lake south of here – about thirty, thirty-five miles away.'

'I thought a lot of them were destroyed,' I said. I seemed to remember reading that they were virtually extinct in the wild state in the USA, although some were preserved in parks such as Yellowstone, and herds of them roam Theodore Roosevelt National Park in North Dakota. The North American buffalo is actually a bison, but tends to be called buffalo by many people. Luther read my thoughts.

'Yes,' he said 'they were practically extinct, but they began programmes to start rebreeding them. Now they're scattered all over quite a bit.'

'What's your Indian name?' I asked him.

'My Indian name is Naganahosh,' he said, barely concealing a mischievous smile that seemed to say, go on, get your tongue around that one.

'You're going to have to spell that one,' Cathy said, laughing. She was taking notes. Luther spelled it out.

'It's a medicine name,' he said. He explained that much 'medicine' in American Indian terms has to do with a sacred bundle, which is made up of secret clan items and other things, such as turtle shell. That bundle has a caretaker within the family and is passed from father to son, and, through secret ritual, prayers and songs, its custodian receives gifts and a special name.

'That's how I got my name,' said Luther. 'It alludes to a horse. This bundle had to do with horses and sacred medicine.' During the rituals, Luther was blessed, in a ceremony meant to bestow on him good luck and protection throughout his life, a good mind and the ability to help his people in whatever problems they have.

'And I'm doing all of that. It just comes natural. I

never even looked for it. It just drops in my lap every time I turn around.'

It struck me that here we were – a family in search of a legend – trying to make a link between this man and a Welsh prince, and here was Luther talking about something that seemed so alien. But such are twists and turns of fortune, and it was an awesome thought that, during those dark days of Welsh troubles more than eight hundred years ago, one man's decision to make a journey would lead to a fork in history. One people would emerge thousands of miles away, carrying with them some of the distinguishing characteristics of physiognomy and language of the Welsh. Mandan culture – impacted by influences of Sioux and other native peoples, and ultimately White America – would develop along its own course, while at home in Wales Welsh too would be susceptible to influences from outside itself.

While the Mandans are said to be of Sioux stock, it's my belief that that influence was part of the life journey of a people – Madoc and his fellow travellers – who began life before they met up with the Sioux and eventually split from them, a people who now like to remember the links with a land far away in both distance and culture from the one they call home.

Luther could see, I think, that my mind was racing, taking in what he had told us about the linguistic links and French explorers, about earth lodges and sacred bundles. He seemed to know what my next question would be.

'Have you heard of the Prince Madoc theory?' I asked. 'That he left Wales and came here?'

'Yes, I believe that,' he said, 'because those Celts, they were in ocean-going vessels. They went all the way around into the Mediterranean area and down the coast of Africa and around England, Scotland and Wales – all around – and they had big tremendous ships.' So it was entirely possible, he seemed to be saying, that they came here, to North America.

'There's a plaque at Mobile Bay in Alabama,' I said, 'saying that Madoc landed there in 1170. Do you know of it?'

'Well, you see, Alabama has a little spur,' said Luther, and he took our map and traced along it with his finger. 'This is Florida, and this is Alabama. Mobile, Alabama, is here. So, anywhere along that coast, all past the Mississippi, there are a lot of bays and bayous. You know, you could land almost any place through there. And according to Verendrye, the French explorer, the Mandans started their journey from around this area.'

Then he gave us the names of three people in the Twin Buttes area who might be of further help. 'Talk to Edwin Benson, Lida Chase or Ernest Stone,' he said. 'They'll set you straight.'

We reminded Luther of our letter from Ed Lone Fight, and asked about him.

'He's part Mandan – he's got more Mandan in him than Hidatsa. See, he's my cousin. His dad's my first cousin. His dad is Ted Lone Fight.'

'Do any of them speak the Mandan language?' Cathy asked.

'I don't think Ed does, but those guys I told you about speak Mandan fluently.'

'Have you got horses?' Matthew suddenly blurted.

Luther smiled. The usual courtesies of conversation were not for a kid. Matthew wanted to ride, and Matthew was determined to mention horses at every available opportunity.

'Yeah,' said Luther. 'I got horses.'

'He said he'd like to ride a horse while we're here,' I offered, half apologetically.

'Well, mine are broncs. Know what that means?' Matthew looked puzzled. 'Well they're wild, and they'll buck you off. I don't have any gentle ones, but I'm working on one. It's too bad I didn't have him tamed already. You could ride him, sure. But he's not tame yet.'

'Who taught you how to ride?' Cathy asked

'My grandpa,' said Luther. 'He was a storyteller, and he had hundreds of stories. I grew up listening to them, when I was a little fella like this guy here.' And with that he ruffled Matthew's hair. 'I didn't know what he was doing to me until I was in World War Two. He was teaching me to be a warrior all those years.

'The basic requisites don't sound like warriorhood at all. It has to do with honesty, courage, being trustworthy, having dignity, honour and respect, and knowing what's truthful and beautiful and fair, and what is happiness and love and so on. And when you have that ingrained into you, then you do not fear death, and that's the warrior's first requisite: not to fear death. Once they spiritually accept that, that there is a life hereafter, in the spiritual world, and it's a better world than we live in now ...'

And Luther proceeded to tell us something about the values instilled into the young in his granddad's day, how youngsters moved through a grade system just as they do in modern American high schools. But this was different.

'Little boys of Matthew's age had their own group.

They had their own costumes, their own paint, their own songs, their own dances and rituals, and the basic thing was honesty and courage. Then, when they got bigger, they went into another study, and they had different costumes and songs and prayers. And after a number of years they went into another stage, but basically it taught the same things: honesty, courage and reverence – reverence for the divine nature of things, courage for the fact that there is another life after death, and honesty to face yourself as you really are, and to have self-control so you won't get guilt and fear. Feeling fear and hate – those things are mental blocks. If you do something wrong and you pick these things up in your mind, you become weaker. You're not as good a warrior then.'

How did Luther feel, I wondered, about being part of a minority now? 'Your people fought very hard for the land,' I said, 'but in the end so many others came here that you just seemed to be outnumbered.'

Luther's face took on an almost melancholy mien as he spoke, slowly, deliberately.

'Yes, disease and genocide, you know. And of course warfare. See, there were thirty thousand of us: there were fifteen thousand Hidatsa and fifteen thousand Mandan. But by the early 1900s there were only eight hundred Hidatsa and two hundred Mandan left. Both together made fewer than a thousand.'

'Because of the fighting?' I asked.

'Some of it.' I thought Luther was about to say something else, so I waited a while before asking my next question.

'What do you mean about genocide?' I asked.

'Genocide. Ah, the government put out infected

blankets,' he said, 'infected with smallpox – out into the tribe. And they got these blankets and they started an epidemic – and they died off from smallpox, 'cause Indians had no resistance to it. Other kinds of diseases, too. You know, like diphtheria – diphtheria was a killer – and typhoid and chickenpox.'

Then, said Luther, were the battles.

'The Hidatsa were with General Gibbin,' he said. 'My grandpa was a scout for General Gibbin, and the Arikara were scouts for General Custer. Now everyone's heard of General George Custer, of course. He led his men into battle at Little Big Horn in Montana.'

'Custer's last stand ...'

'Yeah, that's right. Well, the Mandans, they were with the Hidatsa. They lived together after they moved out of what they now call the Knife River Villages ...' And Luther proceeded to tell me more about the Mandan people, and the other two tribes with whom they share their reservation.

The three tribes and their lifestyle brought a lot of praise from travellers, geographers, fur traders and the like who made contact with them. They were admired for their simple way of life, sedentary, agricultural, proud and noble. They were living prosperously on the prairies – but, because they had settled at a crossroads in the land-seeking white man's empire, innumerable tragedies lay in store for the Mandan tribe. They would be devastated by smallpox and, even in the twentieth century, have their best land inundated by a white man's reservoir.

Perhaps the biggest and most ruinous events in the earlier history of the three tribes and their habitation of North Dakota were the smallpox epidemics. The second and more damaging epidemic struck the three tribes in June 1837 and spread very quickly. In order to escape its effects – or at least to minimise them – the Hidatsa spread along the Little Missouri. The Arikara hovered around Fort Clark. The Mandans, however, remained where they were.

The journals of Francis A. Chandon say that, by 30 September 1837, seven-eighths of the Mandans and half the Hidatsa and Arikara were wiped out. At least one account says the Mandans were reduced from 1,800 in June to twenty-three men, forty women and sixty or seventy young people by the autumn of that year.

There had been an epidemic among the Mandans some seventy years before this. Their numbers had been cut by half and, faced with extinction, the thirty remaining families moved from the mouth of the Heart River, up north to Knife River. They built new lodges and lived partly with one and partly with the other of the two tribes. However, they couldn't agree with the Arikara and by 1839 were living only with the Hidatsa.

Little by little, the three tribes claimed the river and reached Like-a-fish-hook bend by 1844. The date of the permanent union of the three tribes is put at 1862.

The sky had changed since we'd moved out here to talk with Luther. The cold didn't seem to bother him much. I could see that Cathy and the kids were beginning to feel it. But we were all fascinated still to hear this big Indian talk of his people and their friends the Hidatsa and the Arikara, and of the many rocks and boulders along the path of their history.

'Who's the chief now?' I asked.

There are no more chiefs,' he said. 'When they all died off they weren't replaced. The last Mandan chief was named Sitting Crow. He died way back in the 1930s.'

11

Of Princes and Prairies and Present and Past

We had spent hours with Luther, after which he gave us his address and insisted we visit him on our return.

Cathy and I decided to look around with the kids. We crossed the Four Bears Bridge, which spans the Missouri, linking the separate parts of the reservation to each other. Without the bridge they'd be inaccessible to each other - unless you had a boat.

The view around us was spectacular, breathtaking. The rolling hills and never-ending prairie extended far beyond view.

Craig, Matthew and Stacey played on the banks of the Missouri, laughing and chasing each other. How uncomplicated life was for them! How simple their lives compared with those of the Native American children. The natives, I reflected, were torn between Americanisation and sticking with the culture and traditions that linked them with their past, their ancestors. This link now seemed to hang by a thread, celebrated only at certain times of the year. The older generations were desperately trying to hold on to the old ways, trying to make the younger generations see how important their roots are.

Night was drawing near, and we had decided to sleep under canvas. So, in the hired car that just didn't somehow belong in this magical land, we made our way west, deep into the prairie to spend our first night here, in the middle of Indian territory.

Although we'd camped in seclusion on our remote island, here it was different. We had the cold to contend with – but the experience was marvellous. Here I was with my family, camped on one of the last frontiers, listening to the coyotes howling in the background, my mind mingling elements of the present and past, and I thought of the famous plaque in Alabama that seems to say without a doubt that Madoc landed right there in Mobile Bay.

> In memory of Prince Madoc, a Welsh explorer, who landed on the shores of Mobile Bay in 1170 and left behind, with the Indians, the Welsh language.
>
> Authority is
> ~ Encyclopaedia Americana copyright 1918
> ~ Webster's Encyclopaedia
> ~ Richard Hakluyt, 1552 to 1616, a Welsh historian and geographer
> ~ Ridpath's History of the World
> ~ ancient Roman coins found in Forts in Tenn
>
> These Forts resemble the Forts of Wales of the 9th and 10th centuries and of the white Indians of Tennessee and Missouri rivers.

Madoc left his homeland of North Wales and took with him ten ships or more filled with dissatisfied Welsh people

– all eager to begin their lives anew, away from strife and warfare.

Once Madoc had landed in America, his problem would have been finding a suitable settlement for his people. I don't believe they ever did. After making their way through the interior, they tried to settle by cultivating fields and establishing a fine and growing colony, but they were always forced to move from one site to another by savage tribes, leaving behind their very distinctive wigwams, built two feet (a little over half a metre) or more in depth and about thirty or forty feet (9–12 metres) in diameter, and of circular shape. And it was the design of these wigwams that led many to believe that only a people advanced in the arts of civilisation could build in such a way.

The villages the Welsh colonists built were surrounded by walls, which in some places reached twenty or thirty feet (6–9 metres) in height. However, these fortifications – built to protect – finally became a prison for Madoc's people as they were constantly besieged by savage and warlike natives. While many of the group died as provisions ran out, the remainder formed a friendship with the natives.

It's difficult to say exactly when, but the Welsh people amalgamated with the Indians at some point. The next generation of children would have been of mixed race, very likely despised by other tribes because of this. We see much the same sort of racism today – and mixed races get it from both sides. Human nature doesn't really change much!

The mixed races, then, decided to form themselves into a group and moved off up country, where they settled and increased in number and strength. They became known as the Mandans.

Of all the men who spent time with the Mandans, the one who inspires me most is George Catlin, who was born in Pennsylvania in 1796 – one of fourteen children. Like me, he took an early interest in American Indian life. He became a lawyer, but practised for only two years before giving it up to become a portrait painter. In 1831, he visited the American Indians and studied their lifestyles: languages, customs, arts and artefacts, appearance, tools and so on.

Altogether he spent seven years with them, making many notes and sketches. During this time he spent a long period with the Mandans, and his paintings of the Mandan people, especially the women, showed how they differed from other tribes, with their high brows and blue eyes.

Catlin says of the Mandan canoes that they were different from those of other tribes – almost round in shape (just like the Welsh coracle, in fact).

Catlin was convinced the first time he set eyes on them that the Mandan people were a mixture of Native North American and some other race. In his book *North American Indians*, he wrote:

> The Mandans are certainly a very interesting and pleasing people, in their personal appearance and manners, differing in many respects, both in looks and customs, from all other tribes I have seen ... So forcibly have I been struck with the peculiar ease and elegance of these people, together with the diversity of complexions and various colours of their hair and eyes, the singularity of their language and their peculiar customs that I am

convinced that they have sprung from origin other than that of the other North American tribes.

It almost seemed that a Welsh love of the New World was foretold by Madoc's journey. And, in the case of the Mandans, many things the Welsh people had done were carried on their own American traditions: coracles, a way of building homes, jewellery, and other artefacts such as beads and pottery.

The more I learned about the Mandans, the more convinced I became that they are descendants of Madoc and his party of fellow travellers.

That first night camping on the prairie was an experience I'll never forget. The sounds of the animals in the night were exhilarating: enjoyable and just a little frightening. But the below-freezing temperature wasn't easy to contend with. We huddled together for warmth in our small tent, having donned as many clothes as would be comfortable, and eventually we even managed to fall asleep.

In the morning the temperature had risen to about five degrees Celsius, but it felt just as cold. However, it was bright and clear and invigorating.

We packed away our things, got everything into the hired car and set off back to the Tribal Administration Office. We hoped we'd be able to see Ed Lone Fight – the guy who had, after all, sent us the letter inviting us to come.

'Dad,' Matthew pestered as we drove back, 'when are we going to ride some horses?'

'Not sure yet, Math,' I told him. 'We'll try to get something arranged soon.'

'Will I have to go on a horse with you, Mammy?' Stacey asked with a little apprehension.

'Let's just wait and see what we can sort out,' Cathy said.

'OK, Mam. I hope I can, though.'

Cathy laughed.

We did get to see Ed Lone Fight. He's the Tribal Programs Manager, and it was a brief meeting, because he's a very busy man. It's not uncommon for him to be dashing off to Washington, DC, to discuss funding for education, for health programmes or other developments on the reservation. Despite his numerous commitments and duties he still managed to arrange for us to go riding in the Bad Lands. He also introduced us to Harry Sitting Bear, a huge man whose size matches his name – although that's where ursine resemblance ends. And he told us we should visit Clyde Baker, who had heard about our research and had expressed an interest in meeting us.

Harry is a gentle giant, a bespectacled man with his ample grey-black hair tied back in a ponytail, his large face at once welcoming, intelligent and radiating tranquillity.

Harry offered to show us an earth lodge, and we jumped at the chance to see one. The natives don't use these lodges any more. Nowadays the Mandans live in cabin-style houses.

I was quite taken aback by the size of the earth lodge. It was about eight foot high and fifteen foot wide (about

2.5 by 4.5 metres) – and the one we were looking at, according to Harry, was quite small compared with the original Mandan and Hidatsa dwellings.

Then Matthew piped up excitedly: 'Dad, I've seen houses like this – on one of my trips with the school.'

I was stunned. I had never thought to make any comparison between Welsh and Native American architecture. I think what Luther had said about the similarity had washed over all the other information we were having to assimilate, and it hit me now what he'd said, 'That looks like a Celtic-type thing of old, you know.'

'Where did you see that, Math?' I asked.

'I, um, I think it was Castell Henllys ... I'm not sure.'

This was a reference to a reconstructed Iron Age village near Cardigan in West Wales. Matthew had been there on a school trip, in common with thousands of schoolkids. He'd obviously spotted the similarity straightaway.

I turned to Harry. 'Do you think the Mandans are an amalgamation of Native Americans and Welsh people of centuries ago?'

'My great-grandfather on my mother's side was Crow Flies High,' Harry said. 'He had wavy hair and fair skin, and I've heard that Mandan language is different to that of other tribes.'

I showed him some words in Mandan – the ones I'd seen compared to Welsh words – and asked him if they were correct.

'*Maho Peneta* – the Great Spirit,' I said. 'Is that correct?'

'Yes, that's correct,' he said.

I showed him a list of Welsh and Mandan words, and asked him if they were significantly similar.

He studied them for a moment or two, and then a look of surprise shone in his eyes. 'Most of them are,' he said. 'The Mandan and Welsh languages are very similar.'

'Do many native Mandans believe in the Madoc legend?' I asked.

'There could be some truth in it,' he said. 'I mentioned that my great-grandfather, Crow Flies High, had wavy hair and fair skin. Well, his son, my grandfather, had blue eyes; my cousin when he was young had yellow hair, like that' – and he pointed to Craig and Matthew – 'but now his hair is darker. So, somewhere, those traits were introduced into the tribe.'

We left the site of the earth lodge and moved up onto a hillside that gave us a spectacular view over the south side of the reservation. I asked Harry to tell us more about his great-grandfather, Crow Flies High.

'My great-grandfather didn't like what was going on on the reservation,' Harry began. 'There was alcohol, steamboats and gambling. The natives started to lose their Indian ways. So, in 1869, Crow Flies High left with his people and went north – about a hundred and eighty-five of them in all. They consisted of both Mandan and Hidatsa, and they stayed around the Buford and Billings area, which is near Montana. They stayed out here for twenty-five years, before being ordered by the military to leave the area and return to the reservation.

'They were made to walk the whole way, during the month of March, when the weather was cold. Although they agreed to return to Little Knife River, they refused to agree with conditions of the settlement on the individual plots, so in 1894 they eventually settled in the Shell Creek Area.

'My great-grandfather died just four years later.'

'I bet those people could tell a story or two,' I said. 'The experiences they had to endure during their lives.'

Harry gave a little chuckle and put his arm on my shoulder.

'Tony,' he said, 'I think you were born a few hundred years too late.'

'You're not the only one to say that,' Cathy piped up. She had really taken to North Dakota and the reservation. She felt totally at ease with the people and the surroundings. Although she had enjoyed island life to some extent, she seemed to prefer life here.

'Tony,' said Harry as we walked, 'I want you and the family to meet some Mandans. First I will introduce you to Bernice. She's an old lady who will talk to you about her past.'

It happened to be Bernice's seventy-fifth birthday and luckily we had brought gifts, so we were able to give her a tea towel depicting a Welsh woman playing a harp, surrounded by the days and months printed in Welsh.

We all shuffled into her home. There wasn't much room in it. There were three rooms in all: a bedroom, a bathroom and the room in which we stood, looking a little self-conscious. I was thinking how small it looked compared with the spacious earth lodges the people had lived in long ago.

Harry introduced us: 'Cathy, Tony, this is my mom –

not my natural mom, but my mom's sister. My mother died, so my auntie is now my mom.'

'Yes,' Bernice replied. 'And he is my son now. That is our way.'

'Is that the way it's always been?' I asked.

'Yes,' she said, 'always. Please sit down.'

Harry excused himself. 'I have to get back to the administration centre,' he said. 'Meet me back there when you've finished here.' And with that he was gone.

Bernice appraised us all with wise old eyes. I didn't really know how to start, so I came straight to the point:

'Do you mind if we ask you some questions?'

'No', she said, 'I don't mind. You can ask questions.'

'Do you remember much of the old ways?' I asked.

'Yes. I remember when I was eight years old. I lived with my grandmother. She taught me many things. Her language was Mandan – that's all she talked. She was a basket weaver and porcupine-quill worker. She worked with porcupine quills, dying them in different colours. You snip off both sides of a wide flat quill and then you sew them and make pretty designs and fancy work.'

Bernice told us about her tribe's agricultural traditions.

'Some tribes call us the Corn People,' she said, 'because we are agriculture people. We planted gardens and we didn't go anywhere, not like nomads. We didn't do that. We stayed right here along the Missouri river.'

'We saw an earth lodge,' I said. 'You don't live in those any more?'

'Not for a long time now. They were sturdy. We don't move, so we would stay in the village – not like the Sioux.

They would have a small shelter and then move on. We would stay where we were. We would have gardens and store everything in the earth lodge – even our horses and our dogs were inside. All you can see from the outside is in the lodge.'

'Why did you live with your grandmother?' Cathy asked.

'When a young girl gets married her firstborn is given to the grandparents – well, not given exactly, but the grandparents take it, whether it's a boy or a girl. And they will teach this child.'

'Is that just the Mandans?'

'I'm speaking for the Mandans,' she said. 'The grandparents will then raise this child. I was the oldest, so Grandma and Grandpa took me. Mama came to stay with us, but it was always Grandma and Grandpa I had to listen to. Grandma would teach me: "Women don't do this, women don't do that, women have to do this ..."

'But it was different for the boys. I had about six cousins – boys. One was called Lone Bear. Grandpa would teach them games, teach them work outside and teach them how to fish and hunt, and they would have to be real good with arrows. We would have games too – the girls. In fact, I used to have a little ball, decorated with quill work. It was really pretty. And we'd have a cane, too. We'd bounce that ball right here on our feet. I used to have a basket and it had some rocks in it. Today I think they were gold, because they were kinda brownish in colour, and when you scraped them with something sharp they were really shiny.'

'So you could have been playing with some valuable gold?' I asked.

'Yeah. I think it must have been. And we never knew it. But we were not worried about money. We lived without money. We survived off the land. The earth would give to us. We would plant and we'd get berries and we would get animals to eat. We had the river and the springs from the ground. There was no need for money.'

'Were both your grandparents Mandan?' Cathy asked.

'Yes, yes they were.'

'And what about your parents?'

'My father and mother were both Mandan. My father was a big man.'

I thought of Luther Grinnell, and told her about him – how big he was.

'Oh, yeah, but he's skinny. My dad was big, broad.'

I couldn't stifle my urge to smile, and Bernice seemed to know what I was thinking. Luther's one helluva big guy, so her dad must have been a giant.

'Did your grandparents ever tell you stories of their past?' I asked her.

'My grandma told me of when they fetched big stacks of blankets, which all the Indians liked because they were not like the old robes they had. The buffalo robes they had were heavy. Anyhow, these blankets were all from dead people – soldiers. They were infested with smallpox, and they gave these to the Indians.' She was bearing out the story Luther had told us the previous day.

'Was that on purpose?' I asked.

Bernice paused before she spoke, then she said, 'Just to be mean. And many, many died from that smallpox. A whole earth lodge would be infected with that disease. Sometimes they would all die together. My grandmother said those steamboats would come up, and her and her sister, they would sit there, and the soldiers, they would give out things. My grandmother watched. Then they would look for the little kids. They would give them sticks of candy, which was made from molasses. It's sweet, like syrup, but not as good. She said they would pat the kids' heads and say "nice *pupusy*", but she thought they were saying "*ti pupusy*", which means spotted prairie dog. And all along they were saying "pretty *pupusy*". They didn't understand each other. Anyhow, the Mandans called the soldiers "*wasinahorosh*", saying that, they didn't know what they were, so they called them "*mashi*". Today all the white people are known as *mashi*. The white people linked us to the Sioux tribe, because the Sioux language is similar to ours. For water the Sioux say *mahini*, and the Mandans say *mahimi*.

'Going back to what the soldiers did,' I said, 'I suppose it was nothing less than criminal.'

'They demolished the people. They wanted the land. We have been pushed around so many times. If you go by the Rivers Dale and Garrison, and try to cross the water, you will see how big the water is. It's just like a big sea. It's terrible. We just have very little land. We all had gardens – now we don't have gardens. They gave us canned goods – canned food to eat all the time – which isn't good for us. Many natives are diabetic. We didn't have proper food. The river on both sides used to be thick with trees – fruit trees and everything.'

'What happened to the trees?' Cathy asked.

'The army engineers came and cut all the wood off. We didn't have anything,' said Bernice, 'not even a stick for firewood. They cut all the trees, then they flooded the area. They made us all move up to higher ground. Now the whole land is all flooded.'

'I thought this was quite a big reservation,' I said.

'No, it isn't. It's just little compared to what it used to be,' she said. 'When my grandmother was living, when any white people – a minister or doctor or anybody – came toward our cabin, she would tell me to hide. Then she would take a big knife that she had and tell whoever it was that there's nobody here, and you'll have to kill me before you do anything. That's why I never went to school until she died. That was when I was eight. Then they took me to school. They cut my braids off – cut my hair just straight across. Now in our Indian beliefs, if your husband or brother dies in war, that's when you have the right to cut your hair off. But they did that to us.'

'Who cut your hair?' asked Cathy.

'The schoolteachers. And if we spoke our language we got punished or they would starve us. That's why a lot of the younger people don't speak the language today. Well, one thing we keep, I tell you – and that's our religion. Although they baptised us in their churches, we keep our religion. What Grandma and Grandpa teach us, we keep it here.' And she touched her chest. 'What they teach us is instilled in our hearts. It doesn't go away. And today my sons have a sun dance every summer. It would be nice if you could stay for the summer and watch the sun dance.'

'What is the sun dance?' I asked.

'It's our religion. It's our prayers. Menfolk will go out on a high hill and fast for four days and four nights. There's no food, no water: just prayers and offering of smoke to the Great Spirit. Then, after four days, they come down and they go in a sweat lodge for purification. After that they dance to the sun, and you can hear their songs.'

'What do the women do?' Cathy asked.

'They'll help with the cooking. Some will dance too.'

After hearing of Luther's grandfather earlier, I was keen to hear of others and it was fascinating to be talking to someone who had spoken to those who had lived during the last century. So I asked Bernice what her own grandfather was like.

'When my grandfather spoke, we had to listen, because he always said, "Hear me now while my voice is here; tomorrow you may not hear my voice." His Indian name meant "Like a horse" – a white horse that ran swiftly. My grandfather used to tell us about the white men who had the same religion as us, all over the world, but would make fun of us when we went out to fast. But if they opened their minds more, he said, they would see that Abraham went fasting. Moses went fasting – he went up a big mountain and when he came down he was changed. So we do fast, we do have visions, and we're taught different things. And that's something we don't give up.'

Bernice had been a great help, and we'd enjoyed listening to her. We decided it was time to leave her to her thoughts. We thanked her and kissed her on both cheeks.

'You're welcome,' she said. 'I enjoyed talking about the

past.' She gave me a warm smile, then turned her attention to Cathy and the children. She kissed them all before saying, 'You must all try to come back. You will be very welcome.'

12

Blazing Saddles

After our fascinating couple of hours with Bernice, we all had a refreshing night's sleep and awoke with horse riding on our minds. This was the day we'd promised the kids they'd get into the saddle at last.

Ed Lone Fight had given us the name and directions of a ranch where we could find horses. He'd even telephoned the ranch for us, so we were expected.

The ranch was at Killdeer, south of New Town. Cathy and I were a little apprehensive. None of us had ever ridden a horse before. It always looks so easy and natural when you see people on television – especially those who use the horse for transport. I've sat through many a western and other films that show people in the Great Outdoors, and the ease with which they control the animal while remaining firmly – and comfortably – in the saddle.

When the kids had first clamoured for horse riding, and we'd said yes, I suppose I hadn't really thought about it too deeply. If I had I might have had second thoughts. So Cathy and I were a little apprehensive. And yet it would be a journey in time for me. Something of the old Wild West, I suppose. It appealed to the romantic in me.

The children were, of course, excited – and that's

putting it mildly. It was about 120 miles (190 kilometres) to Killdeer and they talked nonstop all the way about what they planned to do once they were on their horses.

We were met at the ranch by Steve – looking the part in denims, cowboy hat and boots. Soon, we were looking at six beautifully groomed horses. Steve, sounding as well as looking like someone straight out of a western movie, took Stacey to a large brown animal.

'Let me introduce you to Honda,' he told her. She turned to us and gave us a puzzled look. But Steve sensed her anxiety.

'You'll be OK,' he said. 'Honda will take good care of you. He's the best we got.'

And with that he lifted her gently into the saddle.

'What's your name?' he asked her.

'Stacey,' came the whispered reply.

'Hey, now, you don't have to be nervous,' he said.

But Stacey just sat stiffly upright in the saddle, which Steve found amusing. However, he eased her nerves with the consummate skill of a doctor telling a patient he was about to have his head removed but everything would be just fine. Really it would.

'See this in front of you, Stacey?' he said. 'It's called the horn. You hold on to it with your left hand, see? Like this.' Stacey silently followed his instructions, visibly calming as she did so.

'With your right hand,' said Steve, 'you hold the reins. Yup, that's right. But don't hold them too tight, now. Leave a little slack. And if you want to stop Honda just pull the reins back gently and say, "Whoa, Honda." And he'll listen to you. OK?'

After he'd patiently shown Stacey the rudiments of equine manipulation, it was Matthew's turn. And Matthew needed no cajoling. He'd waited long and patiently for this adventure, and now his time had arrived. His horse was called Trigger. Whether Trigger was as well trained as Roy Rogers's horse of the same name remained to be seen. Trigger was a beautiful golden colour – almost matching Matthew's hair.

As Steve helped him into the saddle Matthew beamed at us – a small smile first, quickly spreading into a grin. He seemed so pleased with himself.

Then it was Craig's turn. He was just as eager as Matthew (although, being the eldest, he probably thought it wouldn't be the done thing to show too much childlike enthusiasm). Craig was being helped into the saddle of a horse called Doc.

Then Honda – Stacey's mount – decided to make a move. Cathy drew in a breath and held it, her face contorting into something resembling a wince. But her concern was short-lived: Stacey took complete control.

'Whoa, Honda, whoa!' she shouted, entering into the spirit of things with unbounded joy. Honda came to an immediate stop as Stacey pulled on the reins.

'Hey, that's very good, Stacey,' Steve told her, as he ushered Cathy to her horse. Craig and Matthew were by now looking quite relaxed on their mounts – but Cathy, on Molly, was just a little uneasy. Molly had a mind of her own, wandering in all directions. I was reminded of an amusing scene during a stay on our Island when Cathy was adrift in a canoe. It was moving this way and that in the lagoon, and Cathy was unable to control it. Molly was Cathy's dry-land canoe.

I was on Lincoln, who seemed placid enough. All the horses except Trigger – Matthew's horse – were brown of one shade or another. I'm sure there are technical terms for horse colours, but I don't know them.

Food and other belongings were stored in the saddle-bags and we set off. Steve was in the lead, while I brought up the rear. Stacey was close behind Steve, then Cathy, who now seemed to have reached a working arrangement with Molly, and the boys were behind her.

Cathy tried to take some photographs as we began our journey – but Molly seemed to have other ideas. Whether it was the click and whirr of the camera or the fact that Cathy had to take her hands off the reins I don't know, but Molly decided to wander hither and thither and just didn't want to know.

The scenery that confronted us was out of this world. Here was North Dakota spreading out in front of us, behind us and to either side. Vastness induces an excitement in most of us, and this panorama was no exception. Dakota is beautiful country. Forest covers only about one per cent of the land, and trees are to be found mainly near river valleys – oak, ash and cottonwood mostly. There's small red cedar in the Bad Lands, and an abundance of wild flowers grow on the prairie. Then there are several varieties of grass – grama, blue stem, wheat grass – all decorating a terrain speckled with thousands of prairie marshes. At one time herds of bison roamed free all over the prairies of the West. Nowadays they're to be found mainly in parks such as Theodore Roosevelt National Park (which accommodates the Bad Lands), along with elk, antelope, deer, bighorn sheep and wild horses. The national park is split into two units called North and South, spanning more than 70,000 acres. The rugged terrain and vast open spaces are a romantic's dream – a link with those days of Sitting Bull, General Custer, those great American explorers Meriwether Lewis and William Clark, Theodore Roosevelt,

Sakakawea and other legendary figures.

The famous buttes of the Bad Lands are nothing short of spectacular – ranging in colour from a sort of putty yellow to blazing reds.

Although I'm not a birdwatcher, I can understand why people who are go to North Dakota. Twitchers – or birders, as the Americans call them – find it a paradise, I'm sure, with more than 350 species of songbird, shorebird, wading bird, bird of prey, nesting waterfowl. Names such as Western grebe, Ferruginous hawk, Hungarian partridge, sharp-tailed grouse, piping plover, upland sandpiper, Franklin's gull, Sprague's pipit, marbled godwit and chestnut-collared longspur adorn the tourism literature entreating people to sample the ornithological delights.

Then there are the National Grasslands: Sheyenne and Little Missouri. Sheyenne National Grassland is in the southeastern part of the state, and is North Dakota's only stronghold for the greater prairie chicken. In the spring the ardent birdwatcher can see migratory songbirds here, such as vireos, meadowlarks, orioles, sparrows and warblers.

Little Missouri National Grasslands covers 1.2 million acres of prairie and Bad Lands habitats in western North Dakota. Here can be seen mule deer, white-tailed deer, prairie dogs and golden eagles. And they're just a few of the pleasures that await the wildlife enthusiast.

And, if I'm starting to sound like a travel agent's glossy literature, it's because I was so moved by the land I was in – that if I could write poetry I'd have filled several volumes by now!

The state forests – Homen and Turtle mountain – are no less interesting. Here can be found aspen, bur oak, green ash and balsam poplar, which tend to be the home of the

Moose, white-tailed deer, ducks, ruffled grouse and many small animals.

I could go on about the wild beauty and rugged magic of the place – but I won't. Suffice to say that our trip through the Bad Lands was an experience neither Cathy nor I will forget in a hurry. It was an education for our three children that I wish all kids could experience.

As we rode, I couldn't help but reflect on how lucky we were.

'Hold on tight, kids!' Cathy shouted. Steve had guided us over a small trail, and a little to our left was a forty-foot drop. I didn't need Cathy to caution me: Lincoln was already looking over the drop, and I prayed he wasn't feeling suicidal. I gently stroked his neck and told him perhaps it wouldn't be a good idea to jump. As we rode on, the gap between me and the others began to widen as I took in the beauty of the Bad Lands, with its stimulating topography, strange land forms, rocks produced by layers of sandstone, mudstone and black lignite coal.

I nudged Lincoln with my heel, and he went into a canter. I held on – hoping for the best, but I was not at all convinced I'd remain in the saddle for the entire ride. I managed to catch up with Cathy and we rode side by side.

Soon I was back in the rhythm of the ride until Steve announced – as casually as if he were commenting on the weather – that we were about to reach a small ravine.

'And your horses may want to jump it.'

At this point I began to feel a little alarmed. Not only had I not ridden before but also here we were about to leap to our deaths and be battered to a pulp – along with our horses – on a million jagged rocks thousands of feet below.

'So hang on to the reins tightly.'

Steve's voice seemed miles away. All I could think of was this great fissure in the landscape and that I was about to tumble into it. 'What about Stace—' But Cathy's words were cut short as Stacey, now following Steve's example, nudged her horse's side and she was away. We all followed suit. Cathy and I passed Matthew and Craig, who were both grinning from ear to ear, clearly looking forward to the jump ahead. I think I warmed to the idea as the excitement grew. We stopped at a bank. There was a slope. At the bottom lay this two-foot ravine that had worried me so. It was followed by quite a steep stony hill on the other side.

We held our breath. Stacey made her way down the slope. In one swift move her horse had cleared the water in the small ravine and I began mentally to kick myself for my blind panic of just a few short moments before.

Stacey laughed out loud as her horse began to make its way up the slope at the other side. She was obviously enjoying every second of it.

The boys were next – again, swift, smooth, effortless movements carrying them over. Cathy's jump was similar. Then it was my turn. I continued the descent towards the water, waiting for the exhilarating sensation of the jump. The water came closer. Lincoln cantered on.

I held my breath.

I closed my eyes.

Nothing happened.

Lincoln had decided he'd prefer to walk through the water. 'You darn critter,' I wanted to say in my best John Wayne drawl. But I kept my mouth shut and pretended that I had displayed such absolute control over the horse that his decision to saunter through the water had been my own choice all along. I don't think Steve was fooled by my nonchalance, however. Come to that, Cathy and the kids were giving me funny looks, too.

A few hours passed. I had a sore bum, and I suspected Cathy and the kids did, too, but I didn't think it prudent to ask. Cathy rode alongside Stacey, who seemed to be engaged in a deep conversation with Honda, telling him how she wanted to take him home to Wales. She had clearly made a friend.

I rode with the boys. 'When are we going to gallop?' Craig asked – yet again. He had been asking this for the past hour and a half. I changed the subject. I wasn't quite ready for that. Not just yet.

We came to a stop near an escarpment, where there was grass for the horses to graze.

'I wish David was here,' Craig muttered as he dismounted. David and Craig had been through primary school together and David had lived opposite us in Swansea. He was one of thirteen children. His parents had eventually got their wish to move back to their native Ireland – but David was missing his old friends, Craig in particular. And now, in the middle of this great adventure, Craig was missing his old friend, too. While he and Matthew got on well, and we were enjoying ourselves as a family, comfortable in each other's company, he was hankering after some company his own age.

Steve had taken Stacey down from her horse, and she was shaky on her legs. As I got down from Lincoln, I realised that the ride had had the same effect on me – and on Cathy too, she admitted. Only Steve – rugged, gentle and experienced Steve – seemed just the same as he'd been when we'd all mounted up back at the ranch.

When Cathy managed to coax Stacey away from Honda

– where a deep and meaningful conversation was still taking place, if a little one-sided – we sat down and had our sandwiches and something to drink.

Cathy took photos and was just about to switch on the camcorder when Steve called from the edge of the plateau we were on.

'Come and look here – not too close, mind. The drop here's about three thousand feet.'

I'd never seen anything like it. Dry rocky mountains, deep gorges, glistening necklaces of water, ravines and more space than I'd ever seen in one place before. Suddenly I could feel in me the spirit of Crow Flies High – Harry Sitting Bear's great-grandfather – and his people as they celebrated this exhilarating vastness.

It was weird to reflect that people whose line may have originated in my native Wales had looked upon this unchanged beauty down hundreds of years, and had probably felt the same emotions as were touching me now.

Steve, I noticed, was surprisingly quiet. He hadn't talked much throughout our trek. I'd told him of our reasons for being here, of my wish to talk to the people who had, I believed, descended from my Celtic forebears. We discussed the plight of the Native Americans, and he said he sympathised. But that was as much as he said. Although he was our guide, and guided us well, it was almost as though we were on our own now – now that he'd got us all into the saddle and helped us over our initial apprehensions about the ride ahead.

Perhaps that was how he meant it to be.

Soon we were on our way again. Stacey had been the most eager to get back into the saddle – and resume her conversation with Honda.

We came to a large, clear, open patch of land with a mountainous hill in the distance.

'Right, folks,' Steve announced suddenly. 'Time for a gallop. We'll have to gallop now so the horses can get up some speed to get 'em going up that hill over there.'

'What about Stacey?' Cathy asked – her anxiety of earlier returning anew.

'It's OK,' Steve reassured her. 'Honda will take good care of her.' Then to Stacey: 'Hold on now – hold on tight.' And with that he galloped off ahead.

'Oh, no, Tony, look!' Cathy said, not without a note of anguish in her voice, as Stacey bounced up and down in the saddle. If it hadn't been for her feet in the stirrups her whole body would have left the horse. 'She's going to come off, she's going to come off!'

The boys, meanwhile, were well away, whooping and yee-ha-ing. Cathy and I tried to hold back our horses, but they had other ideas. They'd seen Honda and the boys' mounts galloping off towards the hill, and they were not going to be left out. So Lincoln and Molly, without much urging from us, raced on ahead until they caught up with the others.

When we reached the top I could feel my heart pounding. Steve told me that, once one horse starts to gallop, the others generally follow.

I was surprised how easy we'd all adapted to horse riding – but I had to concede that having well-trained horses was half the battle. Molly – Cathy's dry-land canoe of a horse – was a bit of an exception: she seemed to want to stop when it suited her to munch at the grass.

But, in our exhilaration and relief at our survival of this escapade, we were able to forgive her.

13

Troubled Water

It had begun to get dark. Steve stopped his horse and turned to the rest of us.

'We'll camp here for the night, I guess,' he said. 'We can make an early start in the morning.'

As we wearily unsaddled our horses, Steve lit a fire. Although we were tired, not used to riding for long periods as Steve was, I could still feel the excitement in the family that we were about to do what we'd seen a million cowboys do on TV: sit around an open fire at night, under the stars, with the sounds of the prairie around them.

So we sat, with blankets around our shoulders, trying to suck the warmth of the fire into our very bones, as Steve cooked a pile of sausages and a pot of beans. The kids' eyes lit up at the sight of the sausages. Matthew and Stacey wouldn't even look at a baked bean, but they devoured the sausage voraciously and asked for more.

Although we sat under the stars, we didn't have to sleep under them. There were two tents: one for us and the other for Steve. It was cold and we had to snuggle together for warmth, but it wasn't long before we all fell into a well-deserved sleep.

'OK, guys, time to get moving!'

I was jolted out of a peaceful sleep as Steve rapped on the tent flap. Cathy and I got the kids up. We all felt stiff and quite sore. As we emerged yawning and stretching into the crisp Dakota morning, squinting against the light, we saw that Steve had already saddled the horses.

All evidence of our stay here was soon packed away and before we knew it we were making our way to the home of Clyde Baker, the man Harry Sitting Bear had told us about. That didn't take us long.

Clyde's wooden cabin was in the middle of nowhere, surrounded by a white picket fence. Steve took our reins and tied the horses to a nearby wooden rail. 'I'll wait here,' he said, and we made our way up the path and were met by a powerfully built Native American aged about seventy, his wife, Inez, and his granddaughters, nineteen-year-old Meranda and five-year-old Malonie.

'Harry said you wouldn't mind if we asked you a few questions,' I said to Clyde as he directed us to various chairs.

After introductions to his family and preliminary chat about our journey – and how the kids would be boasting about their night under the stars once they got back to Wales – I asked Clyde, 'Do you believe there's a connection between the Welsh and the Mandans?'

He looked at me for a moment, as if composing his answer. But it was a simple direct one: 'Yes, I believe it,' he said. 'Because all the stories I've heard, ever since I was a kid – and I'm seventy years old now – well, ever since I was a child I heard stories that the Mandans, since their history began, have had green or blue eyes and light complexions.'

'Have you always lived in the area?' I asked.

'No, we used to live about forty miles [64 kilometres] down the road.'

'What made you move?'

'Well, it's a long story. See, we moved out of the river bottom to begin with. We were a young married couple then. Well, the government dammed the Missouri river – the Garrison Dam it was called – and flooded us out, so we had to move up to the top.'

Clyde told us about the Garrison Dam, which was started in 1946. Once it was finished, the reservoir covered a massive 155,000 acres (63,000 hectares) of the best farming land on the reservation. The dam had a ruinous effect on the economy of the Fort Berthold reservation, causing the migration of 90 per cent of the reservation people from their lush and fruitful valley land to high ground.

Before the reservoir was built, the reservation had 600,000 acres (243,000 hectares) of land. So the 155,000 acres (63,000 hectares) taken was equivalent to a little over 25.8 per cent.

The dam also separated the reservation into five sections, which are accessible to each other only by driving many miles around. The government supplied no extra land to replace what had been taken, and people were expected to move to higher ground within the boundaries of the reservation, or move off the reservation altogether and find employment elsewhere.

Most of the children went to schools at a place on the reservation called Elbowoods, but this too was inundated by the Garrison Dam. All the children of school age had to change schools when their families were relocated to higher ground. New roads had to be built – about 230 miles (370 kilometres) of them – because the reservoir covered 80 per cent of the existing roads. The new highway was completed in 1954.

Before the dam altered the lives of the Native Americans of Fort Berthold so dramatically, they lived naturally, using springs and creeks for their water supply. They had plenty of wood and exposed coal for fuel, and plenty of timber for all their building needs. Food was plentiful, with wild fruit and animals in abundance.

When they had to move to higher ground, the nature of their economy changed. Water had to come from wells. Wells cost money. Fuel had to be bought. Fuel cost money. The good land was underwater. Now they had to rely far more heavily on money.

'They claim it was for electricity and to irrigate land,' said Clyde bitterly. 'But they only picked on reservation land for these dams. It had the effect of joining the three tribes: they mixed us all up and our way of living was changed.'

'We've been talking to Harry Sitting Bear,' I said. 'He was telling us his father lost good land because of the dam. He was upset because it was his father's land, and he lost it. He told us white settlers came, and he had to move out of his home, too, and now has to live among others with less room to spread out.'

'Yes,' said Clyde knowingly. 'This housing they have today – you may have to live with neighbours you don't really care for. We bought this place. We used to live in town but we didn't like it, so we bought this land. It was better when we lived at the river bottom, before the dam. We lived pretty much with nature then. There was timber, berries and animals. We were very self-sufficient then.

It was good land down there, but not so good up here. We do have a crop up here and some cattle, but it's nothing compared with what we had when I was younger. When we lived down there I never heard the word "welfare". We were independent. We lived altogether different.'

'Are the children losing their old ways?' Cathy asked him.

'Oh, pretty much so,' he said. 'But we're trying to hang on to it, though. The last two generations have been trying to get it back.'

I thought of the Welsh-language campaigners back home. I asked Clyde if the children respected the old ways and wanted to see them return.

'Yes, they want to know where they come from,' he said. 'When I was young, younger than my granddaughter there' – he pointed to Meranda, who was sitting opposite me – 'it wasn't good to be an Indian. We were taught not to speak our native language.'

Where had I heard that before ...?

'I've heard that not many Mandans speak the original language. Is that right?' I asked.

'That's true, sadly,' said Clyde. 'But we're trying to teach the younger people, so we don't lose it altogether.'

I showed Clyde my list of words and asked him to compare the Mandan and the Welsh. He agreed that some words were very similar – too similar for mere coincidence.

'I do think the Mandans originated from the Welsh,' he said.

'What about stories?' I asked. 'Are there any stories told about Madoc?'

'There is one,' said Clyde, rubbing his chin thoughtfully. 'One about the Lone Man. He came here from a land far away. He taught the Mandans about planting and building. There are shrines dedicated to him.'

'And you think this Lone Man was Madoc?'

'I think so,' he said. 'It's very probable.'

During the time we spent with Clyde, we talked of the stories he'd heard as a boy. They were usually about people from a faraway land who came to America and eventually mixed with the natives, thus bringing about the Mandan tribe and its strange language and new skills.

Then Meranda piped up. She'd remained fairly quiet during our conversation, listening carefully and intelligently to my questions and her grandfather's answers. She told us she was proud of her heritage, and talked of what she wanted for her people, and of the traditions that she and others like her strove to keep alive.

Meranda was a dancer. When the tribe celebrated their powwow she would dance the Mandan dances, which are as varied as the bright costumes they wear for the occasion.

'Excuse me a moment,' she said, and disappeared from

the room, only to arrive back a few moments later with one of the dresses she uses for her dancing. It was called a jingle dress, and was covered with hundreds of small metal cones that jingle together with the slightest movement. It was very heavy – I wondered how she managed to walk in it, let alone dance!

While Cathy and I were talking to Clyde, Inez and Meranda about their native lifestyle, our children were busy entertaining Malonie, who was obviously fascinated by these visitors with their funny accent who had come to talk to Grandpa. She was inquisitive, constantly asking questions about the books that Craig was reading her. Stacey was patently quite taken by this other little girl, who was bustling about them.

We were interrupted then by Steve, whom we'd left looking after the horses. He said it would soon be time to go if we were to make it back by nightfall. The conversation with Clyde, Inez and Meranda had been fascinating, and time had flown by. We'd almost forgotten about poor Steve. We thanked Clyde and his family, and were soon back in the saddle – all feeling a bit sore, still, from our mammoth riding stint of the day before.

When we got back to the ranch, the kids were clearly disappointed. They'd loved their horse riding and would dearly love to have done the whole thing again. Cathy and I, from being quite concerned about them when we'd all first got into the saddle and even more so when we'd had to jump the ravine – could see that they would make great riders. Kids are less conscious of safety – especially those of Stacey's age. And they learn better when they're young.

And it was Stacey who was the saddest, at having to leave Honda. She wanted us to take him home with us. But in the end I convinced her that this was the best place for him, with other horses in the open space.

Although our horse-riding adventure was over, our stay in Indian country was only just beginning.

14

The Shrine of the Lone Man

May 1996. We are soon to meet Alan Ereira, a film producer and director, at Minot.

He had heard about my exploits on the Mandan–Madoc link. He was intrigued with the story, and wanted to discuss a proposed documentary. He wanted to do a programme – for transmission in early 1997 – about the theory that other people visited America before Columbus set foot there.

My conviction and research would be at the heart of the programme, he said.

When we met Alan, he was a bit weary after driving four hundred miles (643 kilometres). He walked into the bar of the Ramada Hotel, where we had stayed the night. He was an imposing sight: all six foot of him, with his beard and Stetson. He wore brown sandals and was surrounded by his own cigar smoke.

Alan's something of a historian, and has made many documentaries. He's also written several books, one being *The Elder Brothers*, which is about the Kogi people of the Sierra Nevada range in California, and his experiences of living with them.

'Ah, there you are,' he said as he spotted us at the bar.

Eyeing our drinks, he added, 'Just what I need.' He ordered a Margarita.

'How was your drive down?' I asked.

'Long. But at least the roads were clear.'

We had planned to eat at the Ramada, but Alan suggested going straight to the reservation. We could eat there.

As we entered the reservation I felt a sort of spiritual warmth – especially when I looked behind me at that sign that said: 'YOU ARE NOW LEAVING THE FORT BERTHOLD RESERVATION'. Not yet, I wasn't.

Suddenly I felt relaxed again. Alan laughed when I said I felt as though I were no longer in the United States of America, but somewhere altogether different.

We were booked into the Four Bears Lodge, which is close to the Four Bears Bridge. The lodge is part of the casino. It doesn't exactly enhance its surroundings, but it serves a purpose on the reservation – and plays its part in keeping unemployment down.

The travelling had caught up with us and, after tucking into a meal of steak – steak the way the Americans like it – and all the trimmings, we decided it was time to hit the sack.

We had an 8.30 meeting the next day in the reservation office with Ed Lone Fight, who was there right on time. I made the necessary introductions, and we discussed plans for the documentary.

'I think it's a good idea,' Ed told us as he made notes of our plans in a small book.

'Good,' Alan said brightly. 'I'm so pleased.'

'I think we should go to Mandaree,' Ed said, rising from his seat. 'I've got some people I want you to meet.'

Mandaree, in another part of the reservation, was a forty-minute drive from where we were in New Town. We decided to travel with Ed; Alan followed in the car he'd hired. On our journey towards Mandaree, Ed slowed the car.

'We will have to be silent for a while so that I can show my respect for the sacred bundle,' he said. He prayed for a while, and then threw some tobacco out of the car window. I decided not to ask the significance of all of this. Not just yet, anyhow.

We had our meeting in what Ed called 'the office'. It was a large room with a long table with chairs on two sides at one end, and another, smaller, table at the other end, which held a flask of coffee and some cups.

We were here to meet, for the first time, Louella Youngbear, an elderly Native American, part Mandan. Her daughter, Kathy, who was to become Alan's assistant during our stay, was also there, and we also met two elderly Native American men, Ned and William, and a very European-looking woman called Eunice – but she was Native American. Her Indian name – in English, anyway – was Sweet Grass.

As the meeting was about to begin, our friend Luther Grinnell made a late entrance.

We all turned our attention to Alan, who began explaining what type of filming he was aiming to do, and what he hoped the outcome would be. He would want interviews, he said, and would want to film some of the forthcoming powwow festival. He'd need establishing shots, of course, of the beautiful countryside and parts of the reservation.

I wondered what they were thinking, these people, as this energetic Englishman explained in his very English accent that he wanted to make a film about a seafaring prince who may have been ancestor to both them and the Welsh thousands of miles away.

It had been a successful and enjoyable meeting. We returned to the hotel at Four Bears happy in the knowledge that the natives were very helpful.

Early the next morning, while we were having breakfast, a friend of Alan's whom he'd met on a previous project joined us. She was Joanna, and she had with her a friend and colleague, Maggie, a Native American from the Hopi people. Both had been involved in keeping alive the language of the Hopi tribe, and were here to see if she could do a similar job with the Mandans.

I was reminded of Wales, where classes in our language are held in colleges and community centres throughout the country, attended by native (but non-Welsh-speaking) Welsh people and English incomers alike.

Today we were to visit Edwin Benson at Twin Buttes, with a stopover along the way at Little Knife River. I wanted to show Alan the earth lodge and bullboat.

With Joanna, Maggie and Kathy Youngbear, there was quite a group of us. We travelled in one car with Kathy, while Joanna, Alan and Maggie were in the other.

At Little Knife River, something strange happened. With the memory of Ed Lone Fight's plug of tobacco still vivid in my mind, I now witnessed another act that exemplified the culture of those who seek to preserve what once was. Kathy Youngbear suddenly became quite emotional. She left the path we were walking along and stepped onto the sacred ground where the earth lodges had once stood. This was the last natural settlement of the Mandans, before the smallpox epidemic took hold and caused so much suffering and loss. Fifty or more indents on the ground marked where the lodges of Awatixa village had once stood. Kathy let down her hair and fell to her knees, crying and praying in her native tongue.

Cathy and I could only look on, not quite knowing what to say – or whether we should say anything at all.

When Kathy returned from the piece of sacred ground, she said we had to make an offering. Alan knew immediately what to do. He reached into his ever-dwindling tobacco. Kathy took some and threw it onto the ground on which she had made obeisance in such a dramatic manner. Later she told us she had prayed to the spirits for permission to be there, where so much tragedy had taken place.

Maggie began to share whatever spiritual passions Kathy Youngbear had just expressed, and went over to a small hillock, where she knelt. The rest of us stood in silence.

When the two women had finished praying, they returned to us. 'We have to leave this place now,' said Kathy, who had tears running down her face. 'And don't forget to call your spirits back to you before you get back into your cars.'

On reaching the cars, Cathy asked, 'Why do we have to call our spirits back?'

'If you don't,' Kathy explained, 'they will be left here in limbo.' We did as we were told.

Edwin Benson – who was Kathy Youngbear's uncle – lived in a cabin-style house surrounded by endless prairie. He greeted us warmly and we were pleasantly surprised to see that an abundant feast had been prepared by his wife Eunice in our honour: home-grown corn on the cob, potatoes, home-made beef and vegetable soup, slices of cooked beef that was so tender it fell apart as it was picked up. And to top it all a large slice of home-made apple pie. What else?

After our repast we settled down and spoke to Edwin and Eunice about Alan's plans for the documentary. Edwin told us about old customs, many of them no longer practised. One was the Sun Dance, a ritual in which, years ago, the male natives would puncture their skin. Some would even be hung up by their pierced skin.

I was reminded of that Richard Harris film, *A Man Called Horse*, in which the very same ceremony – subsequently made illegal by the US government – was performed on the hero, played by Harris. It was intended to prove his manhood by displaying his ability to withstand pain. The Harris character, nicknamed Horse, was living among natives and almost became one of them. But he had to prove himself. During the ceremony, sharp claws – possibly those of a bear – were attached to ropes, and then pushed into the skin of his pectorals and secured. As if that were not painful enough, he was then hauled aloft into the roof of the lodge, way up above the central fire.

'Many years ago,' said Edwin, 'when the Sun Dance was performed, a person would chop off one of his arms, and, because the ceremony is very spiritual, the others taking part could pick up the severed arm and attach it back onto the injured man. It would be the same as it was before he had cut it off. Now one year, a man thought he could do better, so he had his head chopped off. But, when the others tried to put the head back on, it wouldn't go, and of course the man was dead. Since then they decided to change the ceremony, and now they call it Okapi, which means "only part".'

Cathy and I looked at each other. Was Edwin joking? Trying to give us a scare?

But Edwin was very knowledgeable about custom and was a highly respected member of the reservation, so maybe there was some truth in the stories. Edwin was one of the few who had a sacred bundle, passed down from father to son within families, and used in religious ceremonies. If the male line is broken, the bundle would be buried with its last custodian.

Edwin's bundle was made of turtle shells and various secret clan items. I was reminded of the bundle Luther had told us about.

Edwin was also keeper of the Lone Man shrine. Clyde Baker had told us about such shrines and Edwin took us out now to an area of quite remote ground where the shrine is situated. We drove some way but the last half a mile had to be on foot, and it was quite a climb. The shrine was a circle of wooden posts, about four feet high. Wrapped around the posts was a band of red cloth intended to mark the level of flood – water, for the Lone Man is a Noah figure.

Stories about him abound, and central to them all is the idea of collecting people and animals on a boat, and the survival of this boat in a flood. I began to wonder if the Lone Man and Madoc were one and the same. You might argue that the Mandans were told this story by others who know the legend of Noah's ark from the Bible. It's also true that similar-sounding stories (virgin births, resurrection and other phenomena) occur in many religious myths and legends, including those of Christianity, and the Noah or Lone Man tale was just one of them. But what makes it odd is that the Lone Man seems to be strictly a Mandan tale, not told by other Native American tribes.

After a fruitful talk with Edwin and Eunice, we left Twin Buttes. I felt that perhaps today I'd moved closer to the shadow of Madoc. The Lone Man was particularly interesting and – who knows? – the arrival of Madoc an his ships could well have been the inspiration for the legend.

Alan was very excited. It had been a very promising day, he said, and we'd be doing most of the filming at Twin Buttes. Preparations were afoot for the forthcoming powwow there, and it seemed that, when it was time to film, a great number of key people would be at Twin Buttes for the celebrations. The powwow is an annual celebration of the Mandans' culture – a festival of music, dance, ritual and ceremonies.

We'd been to see the powwow ground with Kathy Youngbear and her mother Louella.

The site for the powwow just outside Twin Buttes was, as you might imagine, on sacred land. A circular shelter had been erected made up of three sections with entrances between them. For the night-time celebrations, there were huge lights set on poles surrounding the site. A great many people were involved in clearing the site, preparing huts as souvenir stalls and so on.

On our last day of this reconnaissance trip we said our goodbyes to Joanna and Maggie, and then we travelled with Alan south to Bismarck, the capital city of North Dakota, to see what information the museum there had on the Mandans. On our arrival, we met a historian called Richard, who showed us first what was on public display, and then gave us passes to see the archives.

As he showed us down, we stopped by an office and looked at some photographs. Then we met an archaeologist who did his utmost to pour cold water on our research. He told us the Mandans had no connection with the Welsh at all; he knew all there was to know about the tribe, he said.

'What about the stories told by the Mandans of the blue-eyed, blond Indians?' Alan asked.

'A myth,' said our archaeologist, whose name we didn't get. 'Created by the white men and passed on to the Indians.' He believed that Europeans were the only races that could retrace their histories, because they wrote everything down. The Celts and American Indians, on the other hand, related their history by word of mouth. This seemed to convince him that there could never be any worthwhile evidence for a link.

Yet much has been passed on by word of mouth before it got into print – including much in the Bible. I wasn't inclined to take his word, and nor were Cathy and Alan. I'm happy to have an open mind about things, but academics can sometimes show an arrogance borne out of fear of losing the big badge they wear that says in bright shiny letters: 'I AM AN EXPERT, FOLKS'.

Richard interrupted the conversation with the archaeologist.

'I have something that might interest you,' he said. So we followed him into a storeroom filled with antiques: stuffed animals, costumes of various tribes – all very well preserved – Indian jewellery, headdresses, moccasins. They were all packed in drawers and labelled. Then we were shown a scroll, about twenty-five feet (7.5 metres) long, nine inches (23 centimetres) wide. It had been made in 1910 by a Mandan called White Rabbit. He was the last of what the natives called 'scattercorn priests.' They are key figures in fertility rituals – ceremonies at times of planting and harvesting, intended to secure good harvests. We'd been shown pictures of White Rabbit at Edwin Benson's home, and one hung in Edwin's living room.

The scroll was a fascinating piece of Indian history, which gave the lie to our archaeologist friend's claim that only word of mouth was used to pass on historical facts through the generations. It depicted White Rabbit's ancestors through thirty-three generations – all scattercorn priests. All their names were there with their colourful likenesses. White Rabbit had been the one who had completed the scroll, as he had no sons to carry on the tradition. So he took the secrets of scattercorn priests to the grave with him. Interestingly, Lydia Sage, who teaches the Mandan language to old and young, is White Rabbit's granddaughter.

The scroll he made, which has never been published, shows his ancestors going back thirty-three generations – to the time of the Lone Man. If you go back thirty-three generations of British sovereignty, the first corn priest coincides with Henry II – who was King of England at the time when Madoc was supposed to have arrived in America – and that hypothesis seems to fit well with the archaeology.

The scroll is proof that matters that were important to the Indians were recorded, kept safely, and handed down. The written word is not the only way to preserve history. Yes, minor detail might get skewed a little in the telling, but major facts are likely to be preserved, because it is important to the people whose history it is to keep that history faithfully for the benefit of future generations.

It had been an instructive day. The more I chatted to Mandans and other Native Americans, and the more I saw of their culture, the more convinced I became of their succession from our Prince Madoc.

15

Traffic Cops and Thunderstorms

June 1996. We are in Minot again. We picked up the car Alan had hired for us, loaded up the luggage and the children and drove to Bismarck, where we were to meet the rest of the crew. We booked into the Radisson Hotel. The crew was not expected until later in the evening, so it wasn't until the following morning that we met Alan's personal assistant Jill Dales, the sound man Mike Savage, the cameraman Bill Bromfield and his assistant Hugh Adams.

We were excited. Who wouldn't be? We'd had no experience of making a film before, and, while these guys sat around nonchalantly talking of the day's shoot, Cathy and I had to suppress our enthusiasm a bit – adopt an attitude of 'been there, done that, bought the T-shirt' – in case we were thought naïve.

Soon we were on our way. Cathy and I were filmed leaving the Radisson Hotel. It's all so seamless by the time a film reaches the screen, but the amount of preparation that goes into such a simple shot is surprising if you've never been involved before.

Alan would order an establishing shot. This puts what's to come into some sort of perspective. Even such a seemingly simple shot is agonised over, as director and cinematographer discuss angles and lighting. As we would learn throughout the filming procedure, many things would be shot twice. What you eventually see on screen of, say, someone being interviewed and then the interviewer's face nodding is actually shot in two takes – unless you have the luxury of two cameras. Some film makers call it 'doing noddies'. It was odd to think that the nodding interviewers on the evening news and *Wales Today* are just nodding either at a silent interviewee who's had the procedure explained to him, or are nodding into thin air. I wondered why it often looked so false. Now I know.

Anyway, here we were, walking out of the Radisson Hotel into the morning sunlight, trying not to think of the camera watching us with its electronic eye and three or four people standing behind it observing our progress.

Then we were on our way to Little Knife River village, where Cathy and I were to be filmed interviewing Harry Sitting Bear.

We didn't know we passed through a time zone and were an hour earlier than we thought. The village ranger was helpful, giving the children a quiz on the Mandan and Hidatsa, on local flora and fauna, and on native lifestyles. The kids did well. They'd learned a lot already. When they scored high marks, they were issued with ranger badges and certificates.

When Harry arrived, Cathy and I interviewed him in an earth lodge. Harry was sensitive to our apprehension. If walking out of a hotel into sunlight had bothered us, what would conducting an interview be like?

'Don't worry,' said Harry, putting an arm on my shoulder. 'We both feel apprehensive. But we'll see the interview through together.'

I was anxious about something else, though, not just the actual filming and trying not to dry up. I had, through my nosing about in Mandan affairs, brought about this documentary. I wanted it to go well for the Mandans. I was aware, as was Harry, that we were now at the mercy of the film makers. Harry sensed this anxiety, I'm sure.

'There's a purpose to everything,' he said. 'You coming over here, searching. I believe everything will be good. This programme will be a voice for us all.'

'I hope –' I cleared my throat and tried again. 'I hope so.'

The interview went well. Mike, the sound man, remarked afterwards how quiet it was – no fidgeting, throat-clearing, breathing too heavily when not talking, that kind of thing.

I put that down to Harry's natural serenity. I also do quite a lot of meditation, and attention to breathing, as anyone who's ever done it will know, is a vital part of the process. I suppose I've learned to sit calmly over the years and it had come in handy now.

Harry told us – and the camera – about his people, and his thoughts on the link with Prince Madoc, of pride of his ancestors and of the history of the tribes who inhabit the Fort Berthold reservation.

We were booked into a motel in the small town of Halliday, just off the reservation, for the rest of the filming. On our way back there we became part of a scene I've only ever witnessed in the movies. We'd decided on a leisurely journey back, so took one or two detours along country lanes. The kids were in the back of the car; music emanated from the radio; Cathy sang along. The scenery was a joy to behold.

Then I looked into my rear-view mirror and saw the blue and red lights of a patrol car – gaining on us fast. I thought I'd better pull over.

Out stepped a burly cop, leather-garbed and sporting the seemingly compulsory dark glasses. He sauntered towards us, gun holstered to his waist.

'I think he's going to lock us up in one of his cells,' said Matthew, his voice lowered in a mixture of fear and excitement.

'Shush, Math,' Craig hissed.

The officer was now standing by the car door. His voice was dark-brown and rich, as though he were an actor who'd played this part in a movie and decided he'd like to do it as a job.

'Step out of the car, please, and follow me.'

With a badly hidden gulp, I did as I was told, hoping that my Welsh accent and a few smiles would win the day.

He walked to his car and sat inside, motioning for me to look in.

'See that?' He pointed to some sort of display on the screen. 'That's a speed monitor. You were speeding.'

'I was only doing thirty-three,' I protested weakly – and politely.

'The speed limit here is twenty-five,' he said. 'You were doing eight miles per hour over the limit.'

All I could think to do was apologise.

'Where you guys heading?' he asked.

'We're on our way to Halliday. We're staying there.'

'Are you with the English people I passed earlier?'

That must have been Alan and the crew.

'Er, yes.'

'Hmm. Well they were speeding too. Twenty miles an hour over the limit.'

For some reason this made me feel a little easier. My crime was only forty per cent as heinous.

'So what happens now?' I dreaded the answer.

'I'm going to have to fine you,' he said, and handed me a slip of paper. 'Pay within twenty-one days. The address is there.'

I returned to the car heaving a sigh of relief. Four faces gawped at me, wondering what was going to happen. I showed them the slip, and we all burst out laughing.

The next day I stopped off at a post office and paid the fine. It amused me to see that the town near which I had been caught out was Dodge!

It was the evening of the powwow. We could hear the drums, echoing hauntingly all around us. We'd arranged to meet Louella there for a filmed interview. We were getting used to it now – feeling like old hands. Almost.

After my first attempts, all I could say was thanks for the cutting-room floor. I'm sure many of my ahems, ums, ahs and long pauses would end up there. I was trusting Alan and his editor to transform me into a seasoned interviewer, all with the magic of the editing process.

As we approached the site we could see dozens of tents that had been erected there for the festivities. But it didn't look like a good night for a celebration – or an interview. The sky was frowning blackly, and then came the lightning.

We found Louella, and she and Alan decided we'd best do the interview just off the powwow site, somewhere more open where the light was better. So we all trooped off to what turned out to be an ideal spot, giving us a backdrop of spectacular open countryside, with the silver ribbon of a vast river in the distance.

'I should have put on my Indian costume,' said Louella, as Mike checked the sound, and Alan, Bill and Hugh got us into position and did mysterious things with light meters. 'If you come back on Monday, I'll wear it for you.' But we had a schedule to stick to, and the interview had to go on with Louella dressed as she was.

After some preliminary chat, we asked her about a particular story she'd mentioned to us as being part of her folk history – a story of a magic boat.

'A long time ago, there was a boat that took our people from place to place,' she said. 'It was not like any other boat. It was a magic boat that would move by command of your voice. At the head of the boat there was a carved animal head. The people would tell the boat to take them across the river, and the boat would take them. Then it would fetch the others back who wanted to come back to the village. Now there was a young foolish man who did not believe what the others told him about the boat, so he decided to test it for himself. He told the boat to go away, and the boat went. And it never came back. Because no one told it to.'

It was a lesson in faith, we supposed, and in respecting the stories of your ancestors without question.

She told us more about her people, and then Alan signalled for us to wind up. Louella hugged the children, as we were packing. 'I wish these were my grandchildren,' she said.

We thanked Louella for her story and her interview.

'You're very welcome,' she said. 'I know you and Cathy are here to search for the link between our peoples. If there is anything else I can do for you in the future I will.'

'Thanks, Louella,' Cathy and I said in unison.

It was fortunate that we'd filmed when we did. As soon as we got back to the powwow ground, the skies opened. Lightning lacerated the sky and thunder cracked and rumbled. The rain was merciless, stinging in its fury. The celebrations were postponed until the following day.

Disappointed, we drove back towards our motel. The children seemed to think it would be safer there, anyway. They hadn't seen anything quite like this. A mixture of excitement and fear gripped them as they watched the storm through the car windows, and saw lightning hitting the ground quite close by.

I was reminded of Cathy's mother, Brenda. She hates storms.

'Good job she's not here,' I said.

At the first hint of lightning, Brenda would retreat to the safety of the darkest corner she could find. But there was no protection for us, stuck in our hired car with thunder, lightning and rain battling for supremacy all around us.

Then Stacey screamed.

'My God!' said Cathy. 'That nearly hit us. Get us back to the motel. Quick!'

Once within the comparative safety of the motel, we closed the curtains and decided to have an early night.

***

The next day was bright and sunny. It was as though there had never been a storm the night before. We had breakfast in the town, remarking on how it reminded us of something from a fifties road movie. There was a bank, a food store, a post office, the café we were eating in, a couple of bars. And that was about it. Far from finding it tatty, we thought it thoroughly charming and evocative.

Our next interview was to be with Edwin Benson. So we all went off to the powwow site to pick him up. He took us back to the Lone Man Shrine – way out in the wilderness.

Edwin made an offering of tobacco – pushing it into the circle inside the wooden posts – and said a prayer in his native tongue. During the interview, Edwin told us again about the Lone Man legend, how he had come from far away and taught the Mandans about building and planting. We would find out more about the Lone Man in our interview with Ed Lone Fight the following day, but for now we all went back to the powwow site – and a feast that awaited us.

We'd been invited to join the rest of the spectators – including the Governor of North Dakota, Ed Schafer, and his wife Nancy – and the powwow participants in the most abundant feast of beef, potatoes, beans, pasta and a host of other things.

Colourful, energetic dancing by the young natives in dazzling costumes enlivened the day even further. All of them were handmade, and some must have taken weeks to create.

Although we were here doing research and helping to make a documentary, we couldn't resist entering into the spirit of things like typical tourists, and taking a lot of photographs for our album.

It was against the background of the Kildeer Mountains that we were to interview Ed Lone Fight. We crossed some fields until we came to the edge of a cliff overlooking the mountain view. The peaks seemed to go on for ever.

'Did all the land we see around us once belong to the three tribes?' I asked Ed by way of an opener.

'Yes,' he said. 'All this was our land, but due to the dam and the government our lands have been greatly reduced.'

We moved on to the Lone Man legend, and Cathy asked if it was peculiar to the Mandan people.

'Yes, that story is what sets the Mandans apart from other tribes,' he said. 'The Mandans talk of the Lone Man, while other tribes talk of the Creator. There is a difference in the tales. The Lone Man is said to be the creator of cattle – among other things – while the Creator created buffalo. Maybe that is the link you are looking for. The Lone Man stories are about European cattle, while other tribes talk of buffalo.'

'What do you think of the idea of being connected to the Welsh?' I asked. 'And do the Mandans accept the legend?'

Without evading my question, Ed said there were many things in the Mandans' history that concerned him, and the smallpox epidemics had wiped out many people, and much oral tradition. 'But the connection is always there,' he said. 'We accept it as part of our lives. My grandfather, you know, had a spot of ginger hair on his head.'

It was as if the argument had been clinched once and for all.

The next stars of our documentary were to be the buffalo that had played such a large part in the lives of the Plains Indians for so many centuries. First we had to find them.

We drove past Mandaree to Skunk Creek Bay – a place with the sort of name I thought I'd only ever encounter in a western movie. The herd belongs to the three tribes and roams hundreds of acres of land at the edge of a lake.

Bob, who looked after the herd, helped us. He opened a large gate that was chained shut, and we all drove through. After a sharp turn to the left we found ourselves almost hidden by grass. Only tyre tracks enabled us to see where we were going.

As we bumped over humps and screeched across small ditches, the kids thought we were filming for a James Bond film rather than a TV documentary, and we were in hot pursuit of villains. When we got out of our vehicles, I turned to Mike the sound man, and commented, 'No one would treat their own cars like that.'

'Don't worry,' he said. 'They're only hire cars.'

Suddenly Bob shouted, 'There!' We all looked, and saw some of the herd grazing peacefully near a gully. The fact that there were only a few of them brought home to me the way these animals, too, had been reduced to such pitifully small numbers by the march of time and 'progress'. I was reminded of that spectacular scene from the Kevin Costner movie *Dances with Wolves*, in which the buffalo in their hundreds, maybe thousands, thundered across the screen. And here were a handful of them, grazing contentedly, looking quite harmless and almost cuddly.

Yet, like the Mandans, they had survived, and also looked proud and noble as they grazed.

Bill the cameraman and his assistant Hugh managed to get quite close for a while, filming them as they grazed. Then the great creatures became uneasy and stampeded away down into the valley.

While the crew were packing away their gear, and Cathy and I took some photos of the view, Matthew ran up to us full of excitement clutching some object whose origin we could only guess at.

'Look,' he said. 'Look what Bob gave me.' In his hand was a large tooth. 'It's a buffalo tooth,' he said proudly. 'And I'm taking it home.'

The next day was to be our last day filming in the US. We were to interview Kathy Youngbear – and again we would be at the powwow ground. The place was almost deserted now the celebrations were over. A few tents remained, but their owners were taking them down and preparing to go. A few scavenging birds scoured the ground for any titbits that had been dropped during the weekend's festivities.

Kathy Youngbear was wearing her hair in a ponytail, and wore sunglasses to hide eyes swollen by being out in the sun for too long. The weekend in the open, and the Sun Dance, had left their mark.

I was impressed by Kathy's performance during the interview. It was as though she'd done this sort of thing before – and maybe she had. Her voice was strong and confident, that of someone who had something to say. And this interview was about to turn into one of the more remarkable of our time filming, because of what Kathy said to us.

First, she spoke of the arrival of Columbus, which she saw as the start of the unwelcome European invasion of her native land. At one point, quite surprisingly, she paused and turned to Alan.

'Have you got any of those cigars you smoke to spare?' she asked.

'Yes,' he said taken aback.

'They smell nice,' said Kathy. 'I'd like to try one.'

'OK,' said Alan. 'I'll let you have a packet after the interview. And we resumed. Kathy turned back to the camera and talked of how her ancestors were light-skinned and fair-haired. Then she turned to face Cathy and me, and said, 'I've got to know you two personally, and I believe you people are doing a good thing. I wasn't sure what you expected when I first met you. You were just some white people who wanted something from us. But now I know you are honest genuine people, and I feel a bond with you.'

Her words made me feel proud. These people, I reflected, had every right to be suspicious of outsiders after all they'd been through – and were still going through – today. To have gained their trust like this was a great honour. I could understand why Cathy loved this part of America and its people: they were kind, likable, honest people and their warmth was quite overwhelming.

Our day of filming had come to an end. We hugged Kathy Youngbear – although there was one final thing she'd be doing for us. She was to guide Alan and the crew to Edwin Benson's house to get a shot of the picture of White Rabbit, which hung on the wall at his home.

16

The Heat is On

We headed back to Mandaree, where Georgia Fox lived. We'd met her briefly during our first visit with Alan. She'd invited my family and me to partake of the sweat lodge.

Craig was a little apprehensive. 'What if we see spirits?' He asked.

Matthew, on the other hand, wanted to see something supernatural if the opportunity presented itself.

We pulled up outside Georgia's trailer home. She must have heard us, because she came out to greet us. Georgia and her sister Nina live in the trailer with Georgia's little daughter Sky. Georgia was in her late thirties, and sported long black hair, which she wore tied back.

Sky couldn't wait to get Stacey inside, to have another little girl to play with. 'Do you want to come play with me?' she asked. Stacey didn't need a second invitation. So off they went at a nod from Cathy and me, and disappeared into the trailer.

'The lodge isn't quite ready yet,' said Georgia. 'Why don't you come inside and wait?'

We followed Georgia up the steps. At the top lay a

husky dog that looked like a cuddly bear. There were also puppies running around, excited by the welcome interruption to their routine.

The inside of the trailer looked a lot bigger than the outside. We were introduced to Nina, who was slightly older than Georgia but very similar in looks. We had brought some tobacco and a red cloth as an offering. Cathy gave them to Nina, who was going to the lodge to prepare it for the sweat.

Sweating is one of the many ceremonies that are common to Native American tribes, varying only in detail. The lodge is like a sauna, and water is poured over hot stones to create cleansing steam.

'Tony,' said Georgia, 'you and the boys can come and help me pick some white sage. We need quite a lot for the sweat.'

Cathy remained in the trailer with Nina and Georgia's mother, who lived in a cabin-style house next to the home of her daughters. Nina showed her some of the quilts her mother made – beautiful and spectacular things, decorated with wolf and buffalo designs.

After we'd collected the sage, Georgia, the boys and I took the bundles to the lodge, which was a wooden, arched frame covered by canvas and blankets. A buffalo skull was placed at the entrance.

Nina was there already, with Cathy, and was shovelling hot sandstones from a large pit that stood close by. The stones are heated for hours in the pit and then placed into a smaller pit inside the lodge.

Objects needed for the sweat were placed just outside the entrance. Beside the tobacco and red cloth we had brought were a pipe and crystal stone.

'Dad, Mum's got to take all her clothes off,' said Craig.

'What?' I said. 'She's going in naked?'

'I don't know,' said Craig, highly amused by the whole business, 'but she's looking embarrassed.'

Then Cathy appeared. She wasn't naked, but wore a very long and old T-shirt that had lots of holes in it. She looked for all the world like a war-torn refugee.

'Craig said you were going in naked,' I said, winking at my son. Cathy said nothing but gave me one of those 'what have you got me into now?' sort of looks.

Nina had overheard Craig's and my conversation. 'Yes,' she said, 'women do usually go in naked, but because you and the boys are going in we'll be wearing something.'

'Oh', was all I could think of to say, glad to be relieved of any possibility of embarrassment.

'By the way,' said Nina, 'rings or any other metal you're wearing will have to be taken off. They'll get so hot in there they'll burn you.'

Once the stones were inside the lodge, the heat from them could be felt even outside. I began to wonder what the heat would be like on the inside. My chance to find out came as we were invited to step inside, from the left-hand side, on our hands and knees. We had been instructed to say – as a mark of respect to our ancestors – 'All our relatives' as we entered. It had also been explained to us that there would be three sittings and the lodge would therefore be opened twice during the ceremony. This would allow those who felt a little overcooked to get out into the cooler air.

Eight of us were taking part: my family and I and Georgia, Nina and Sky. Once inside the lodge, we noticed that the sage we'd picked was scattered on the floor. There were blankets on the floor, too, for us to sit on, and hanging on the frame of the lodge was a piece of red cloth, some sage and a buffalo skull.

We sat in a circle around the pit. Georgia closed the entrance and the room went black as night – and very hot very quickly.

'Mammy, I don't like it,' Stacey moaned pitifully from the opposite side to me. Georgia asked her, 'Do you want to go out, Stacey?'

'Yes.'

So the entrance was opened and Stacey crawled out – much faster than she had crawled in.

'If any of you get too hot,' said Nina, 'lie on the floor. It's a little cooler there.'

The entrance was then closed once more. Within minutes the boys were lying down. Nina was praying and giving thanks to God and the spirits of her ancestors. In the blackness, sweating profusely, hearing Nina's soft-spoken words of prayer in her own tongue, I found my mind wandering back to the reason we were here: our Madoc–Mandan link. It was only the offer of a drink of water from a buffalo horn that brought me round.

I don't know how long I'd sat, sedated by the hypnotic quality of my surroundings.

'Tony,' said Nina, 'take this. Put some on your head, on your eyes, on all your body if you want to. And drink some. What you don't use, throw on the stones.'

I did as Nina told me. Even though the water had become warm in the stiflingly hot atmosphere, it nevertheless seemed cool and refreshing by comparison. As I threw the water on the stones, the heat rose dramatically, and the room seemed even hotter.

Eventually, it was time to open the entrance for the first time. Cathy, the boys and I were keen to get some cool air into our lungs. Outside the sun seemed a thousand times brighter than it had before we'd gone in. The breeze was cooling and very welcome, and we drank thirstily from bottled water we'd brought with us. Cathy's torn T-shirt was clinging to her body, wet with sweat.

We were one down for the second sitting: Sky had decided she didn't want to go back in. She wanted to remain outside and play with Stacey.

During the sweating we took turns to give thanks for our newfound friends, and asked for strength to be given to any family or friends who might be ill or suffering.

Georgia and Nina then offered more prayers, both in English and their native tongue.

During the third sitting the pipe was lit. Now I'm not the fanciful type when it comes to visions and things, but – and I'm not sure whether this was the effect of the heat, the smoke from the pipe or both – I swear I saw the head of a wolf. Matthew hadn't used the pipe, but swore he'd seen a fish.

After the third session we once again crawled out into the welcoming cool air, feeling light and relaxed. Back at the trailer we were entertained to a buffet of sliced meats, bread rolls, crisps – or potato chips, as our hosts call them – cheese and various other tasty titbits. All that sweating had given us an appetite.

After we'd eaten, Georgia announced, 'I've got something for you all.' She disappeared into her bedroom and emerged with some feathers. She handed a large one to Cathy and me, and some smaller ones to the children.

'They're eagle feathers,' she explained. 'They're held by the tribe to be sacred symbols, and it's considered an honour to be given them. An honour not bestowed on many whites,' she added.

The time came for us to take our leave once more of Fort Berthold reservation and its people. We were sorry to say goodbye.

Before we left America we did some shopping at the mall in Minot. The children had lists of friends and teachers they wanted to take gifts to. Matthew's teacher, Mr Sanders, has himself travelled through Dakota – South, though, not North – and was keen for Matthew to share his experiences with the class.

Craig, whose GCSE exams were getting closer, felt he had done enough globetrotting for the time being. He always took a pile of books with him on our travels, but he was keen now to get back to studying in a more conventional way – in a school. There would be plenty of time for travelling. Soon we were driving away from Fort Berthold, and I realised that I was the only one awake, which was just as well because I was at the wheel. Our stay here was at an end.

It took a while for Cathy and the children to readjust to life in Swansea. Cathy made her weekly trips to Tesco, Craig got into his studies and Matthew and Stacey talked constantly to their friends about their adventures. As for me – well I couldn't get rid of the thoughts of warm sand between my toes, and the smell of the tropical air. Wanderlust was beckoning me back to the South Seas.

Within months my family agreed to let me go.

For the first time since our marriage we would be separated.

Epilogue

Miari posed by the hibiscus tree. The red flowers were in full bloom. We had left the tiny islet – the *motu* – and were now back at my place on Rarotonga.

The sun was at its peak as we both took turns in posing for photos. I didn't really like having my picture taken – but Miari was a natural.

'You've done this before,' I said jokingly.

'I have actually,' she replied. 'When I was in New Zealand I went out with this *papaa*. He was a teacher at a school I used to go to. He told me he was thirty-six. I told him I was twenty-seven, and I was only twenty. And then, as soon as I turned twenty-one, I told him I was twenty-one. And then he told me that he was thirty-nine or something – but then over the phone I heard him have a conversation and he admitted he was forty-two, and I thought that was really old, especially since I was such a young age.

'But then he was quite a weird guy. He was into this Polynesian-girl mode, he'd call it "*wahini*". He loved the *wahini*. He used to take pictures of me wearing those head *eis* [headdresses] – you know, made of flowers. He would have me stand sideways, kinda half naked. Yeah, so he was too kinky for me, and I wasn't into that kind of stuff because I didn't know what he was doing. I was only topless though – I had my *pareu* on and my hair covering my breasts. They were black-and-white shots. I still want to get those pictures. They were quite nice actually, as I remember. But he was a bit of a weirdo – so I left a letter and went back to the Cook Islands.'

Miari placed a flower behind my ear, and we sat talking for a while.

'I'm going into town,' she suddenly announced. 'I'll get some food – and I need to check the post office for any letters.' She started her bike, and was gone.

I was lost in utopia – my obsession with Polynesian life made me forget time. It wasn't long before Miari returned – with a letter addressed to me. It was from Cathy. I hadn't realised it had been three months since I had seen my family. Cathy said in her letter she missed me and was coming over – to spend some time with me and eventually take me back to Swansea and the children.